Django for APIs

Build web APIs with Python and Django

William S. Vincent

Django for APIs

Build web APIs with Python and Django

William S. Vincent

learndjango.com

ISBN-13: 978-1735467221

Also By William S. Vincent

Django for Beginners

Django for Professionals

Contents

Introduction

In this book you will learn how to build multiple web APIs of increasing complexity using Django and Django REST Framework. Django is a very popular Python-based web framework that handles the challenging parts of building a website: authentication, connecting to a database, logic, security, and so on. There are also thousands of third-party packages that add functionality to Django itself, the most prominent of which is Django REST Framework, which allows developers to transform any existing Django project into a powerful web API.

Django and Django REST Framework are used by the largest tech companies in the world, including Instagram, Mozilla, and Pinterest. But they are also well-suited to beginners or weekend side projects because Django's "batteries-included" approach masks much of the underlying complexity, allowing for rapid and secure development. By the end of this book you will be able to create production-ready web APIs with a small amount of code in an even smaller amount of time.

Why APIs

An API (*Application Programming Interface*) is a shorthand way to describe how two computers communicate directly with one another. For web APIs, which exist on the world wide web, the dominant architectural pattern is know as REST (*REpresentational State Transfer*) and will be covered properly later on in this book.

Back in 2005, when Django was first released, most websites consisted of one large monolithic codebase. The back-end of database models, views, and URLs were combined with front-end templates to control the presentational layer of each web page.

But these days it is far more common for websites to adopt an API-first approach of formally separating the back-end from the front-end. This allows a website to use a dedicated JavaScript front-end framework, such as React or Vue, which were released in 2013 and 2014 respectively.

When the current front-end frameworks are eventually replaced by even newer ones in the years to come, the back-end API can remain the same. No major rewrite is required.

Another major benefit is that one single API can support multiple front-ends written in different languages and frameworks. Consider that JavaScript is used for web front-ends, while Android apps require the Java programming language, and iOS apps need the Swift programming language. With a traditional monolithic approach, a Django website cannot support these various front-ends. But with an internal API, all three can communicate with the same underlying database back-end!

Growing websites can also benefit from creating an external API that allows third-party developers to build their own iOS or Android apps. When I worked at Quizlet back in 2010 we did not have the resources to develop our own iOS or Android apps, but we *did* have an external API available that more than 30 developers used to create their own flashcard apps powered by the Quizlet database. Several of these apps were downloaded over a million times, enriching the developers and increasing the reach of Quizlet at the same time.

The major downside to an API-first approach is that it requires more configuration than a traditional Django application. However as we will see in this book, the fantastic Django REST Framework library removes much of that complexity for us.

Django REST Framework

There are thousands of third-party apps available that add further functionality to Django. You can see a complete, searchable list over at Django Packages[1], as well as a curated list in the awesome-django repo[2]. However, amongst all third-party applications, Django REST Framework is arguably **the** killer app for Django. It is mature, full of features, customizable, testable, and extremely well-documented. It also purposefully mimics many of Django's traditional conventions, which makes learning it much faster. If you already know Django, then learning Django REST Framework is the logical next step.

---

[1]https://djangopackages.org/
[2]https://github.com/wsvincent/awesome-django

Prerequisites

If you're brand new to web development with Django, I recommend starting with my book Django for Beginners[3]. The first several chapters are available for free online and cover proper set up, a *Hello World* app, a *Pages* app, and a *Message Board* app. The full-length version goes deeper and covers a *Blog* website with forms and user accounts as well as a production-ready *Newspaper* site that features a custom user model, complete user authentication flow, emails, permissions, deployment, environment variables, and more.

This background in traditional Django is important since Django REST Framework deliberately mimics many Django conventions. It is also recommended that readers have a basic knowledge of Python itself. Truly mastering Python takes years, but with just a little bit of knowledge you can dive right in and start building things.

Why this book

I wrote this book because there is a distinct lack of good resources available for developers new to Django REST Framework. The assumption seems to be that everyone already knows all about APIs, HTTP, REST, and the like. My own journey in learning how to build web APIs was frustrating... and I already knew Django well enough to write a book on it! This book is the guide I wish existed when starting out with Django REST Framework.

Chapter 1 covers the initial set up of installing Python, Django, Git, and working with the command line. **Chapter 2** is an introduction to web APIs and the HTTP protocol that underpins it all. In **Chapters 3-4** we review the differences between traditional Django and Django REST Framework by building out a *Library* book website, transforming it into an API, adding tests, and then deploying it live. In **Chapter 5** we build, test, and deploy a *Todo* API with list and detail API endpoints. It also includes Cross Origin Resource Sharing (CORS).

Chapter 6 is the start of a making a production-ready *Blog* API that uses a custom user model and full Create-Read-Update-Delete (CRUD) functionality. **Chapters 7** focuses on permissions, how to limit access appropriately, and creating a custom permission class. In **Chapter 8** the

---

[3]https://djangoforbeginners.com/

focus turns to user authentication and the four built-in authentication methods. Then we add endpoints for user registration, log out, password reset, and password reset confirmed. **Chapter 9** turns to viewsets and routers, built-in components that can greatly reduce the amount of coding required for standard API endpoints. **Chapter 10** covers schema and documentation and **Chapter 11** goes step-by-step through a production deployment.

Complete source code for all chapters can be found online on Github[4].

Conclusion

Django and Django REST Framework is a powerful and accessible way to build web APIs. By the end of this book you will be able to add APIs to any existing Django projects or build your own dedicated web API from scratch properly using modern best practices. Let's begin!

---

[4]https://github.com/wsvincent/restapiswithdjango

Chapter 1: Initial Set Up

If you have already read Django for Beginners[5] much of this will be familiar but there are additional steps around installing Django REST Framework.

This chapter covers how to properly configure your Windows or macOS computer to work on Django projects. We will start by reviewing the *Command Line*, a powerful text-only interface that developers use extensively to install and configure software projects. Then we install the latest version of Python, learn how to create dedicated virtual environments, and install Django. As a final step, we will explore using Git for version control and working with a text editor. By the end of this chapter you will have created your first Django and Django REST Framework project from scratch. In the future, you will be able to create or modify any Django project in just a few keystrokes.

The Command Line

The command line is a text-only interface that harkens back to the original days of computing. It is an alternative to the mouse or finger-based graphical user interface familiar to most computer users. An everyday computer user will never need to use the command line but software developers do because certain tasks can only be done with it. These include running programs, installing software, using Git for version control, or connecting to servers in the cloud. With a little practice, most developers find that the command line is actually a faster and more powerful way to navigate and control a computer.

Given its minimal user interface–just a blank screen and a blinking cursor–the command line is intimidating to newcomers. There is often no feedback after a command has run and it is possible to wipe the contents of an entire computer with a single command if you're not careful: no warning will pop up! As a result, the command line must be used with caution. Make sure

---

[5]https://djangoforbeginners.com

not to blindly copy and paste commands you find online; only rely on trusted resources for any command you do not fully understand.

In practice, multiple terms are used to refer to the command line: Command Line Interface (CLI), console, terminal, shell, or prompt. Technically speaking, the *terminal* is the program that opens up a new window to access the command line, a *console* is a text-based application, the *shell* is the program that runs commands on the underlying operating system, and the *prompt* is where commands are typed and run. It is easy to be confused by these terms initially but they all essentially mean the same thing: the command line is where we run and execute text-only commands on our computer.

On Windows, the built-in terminal and shell are both called *PowerShell*. To access it, locate the taskbar on the bottom of the screen next to the Windows button and type in "powershell" to launch the app. It will open a new window with a dark blue background and a blinking cursor after the > prompt. Here is how it looks on my computer.

Shell

```
PS C:\Users\wsv>
```

Before the prompt is PS which refers to PowerShell, the initial C directory of the Windows operating system, followed by the Users directory and the current user which, on my personal computers, is wsv. Your username will obviously be different. At this point, don't worry about what comes to the left of the > prompt: it varies depending on each computer and can be customized at a later date. The shorter prompt of > will be used going forward for Windows.

On macOS, the built-in terminal is called appropriately enough *Terminal*. It can be opened via Spotlight: press the Command and space bar keys at the same time and then type in "terminal." Alternatively, open a new Finder window, navigate to the *Applications* directory, scroll down to open the *Utilities* directory, and double-click the application called Terminal. This opens a new screen with a white background by default and a blinking cursor after the % prompt. Don't worry about what comes to the left of the % prompt. It varies by computer and can be customized later on.

Shell

```
Wills-Macbook-Pro:~ wsv%
```

If your macOS prompt is $ instead of % that means you are using Bash as the shell. Starting in 2019, macOS switched from *Bash* to *zsh* as the default shell. While most of the commands in this book will work interchangeably, it is recommended to look up online how to change to zsh via System Preferences if your computer still uses Bash.

Shell Commands

There are many available shell commands but most developers rely on the same handful over and over again and look up more complicated ones as needed.

In many cases, the commands for Windows (PowerShell) and macOS are similar. For example, the command whoami returns the computer name/username on Windows and just the username on macOS. As with all shell commands, type the command itself followed by the return key. Note that the # symbol represents a comment and will not be executed on the command line.

Shell

```
# Windows
> whoami
wsv2021/wsv

# macOS
% whoami
wsv
```

Sometimes, however, the shell commands on Windows and macOS are completely different. A good example is the command for outputting a basic "Hello, World!" message to the console. On Windows the command is Write-Host while on macOS the command is echo.

Shell

```
# Windows
> Write-Host "Hello, World!"
Hello, World!

# macOS
% echo "Hello, World!"
Hello, World!
```

A frequent task on the command line is navigating within the computer filesystem. On Windows and macOS the command pwd (print working directory) shows the current location.

Shell

```
# Windows
> pwd

Path
----
C:\Users\wsv

# macOS
% pwd
/Users/wsv
```

You can save your Django code anywhere you like but for convenience we will place our code the desktop directory. The command cd (change directory) followed by the intended location works on both systems.

Shell

```
# Windows
> cd onedrive\desktop
> pwd

Path
----
C:\Users\wsv\onedrive\desktop

# macOS
% cd desktop
% pwd
/Users/wsv/desktop
```

Tip: The `tab` key will autocomplete a command so if you type `cd d` and then hit `tab` it will automatically fill in the rest of the name. If there are more than two directories that start with `d`, hit the `tab` key again to cycle through them.

To make a new directory use the command `mkdir` followed by the name. We will create one called `code` on the Desktop and then within it a new directory called `setup`.

Shell

```
# Windows
> mkdir code
> cd code
> mkdir setup
> cd setup

# macOS
% mkdir code
% cd code
% mkdir setup
% cd setup
```

You can check that it has been created by looking on your Desktop or running the command `ls`. The full Windows output is slightly longer but is shortened here for conciseness.

Shell

```
# Windows
> ls
setup

# macOS
% ls
setup
```

Tip: The clear command will clear the Terminal of past commands and outputs so you have a clean slate. The tab command autocompletes the line as we've discussed. And the ↑ and ↓ keys cycle through previous commands to save yourself from typing the same thing over and over again.

To exit you could close the Terminal with your mouse but the hacker way is to use use the shell command exit instead. This works by default on Windows but on macOS the Terminal preferences need to be changed. At the top of the screen click on Terminal, then Preferences from the drop down menu. Click on Profiles in the top menu and then Shell from the list below. There is a radio button for "When the shell exits:". Select "Close the window."

Shell

```
# Windows
> exit

# macOS
% exit
```

Kinda cool, right? With practice, the command line is a far more efficient way to navigate and operate your computer than using a mouse. For this book you don't need to be a command line expert: I will provide the exact instructions to run each time. But if you are curious, a complete list of shell commands for each operating system can be found over at ss64.com.

Install Python 3 on Windows

On Windows, Microsoft hosts a community release of Python 3 in the Microsoft Store. In the search bar on the bottom of your screen type in "python" and click on the best match result.

This will automatically launch Python 3.10 on the Microsoft Store. Click on the blue "Get" button to download it.

To confirm Python was installed correctly, open a new Terminal window with PowerShell and then type `python --version`.

Shell

```
> python --version
Python 3.10.2
```

The result should be at least Python 3.10. Then type `python` to open the Python interpreter from the command line shell.

Shell

```
> python
Python 3.10.2 (tags/v3.10.2:a58ebcc, Jan 17 2022, 19:00:18)
[MSC v.1929 64 bit (AMD64)] on win32
Type "help", "copyright", "credits", or "license" for more information.
>>>
```

Install Python 3 on Mac

On Mac, the official installer on the Python website is the best approach. In a new browser window go the Python downloads page[6] and click on the button underneath the text "Download the latest version for Mac OS X." As of this writing, that is Python 3.10. The package will be in your `Downloads` directory. Double click on it which launches the Python Installer and follow through the prompts.

To confirm the download was successful, open up a new Terminal window and type `python3 --version`.

---

[6]https://www.python.org/downloads/

Shell

```
% python3 --version
Python 3.10.2
```

The result should be at least 3.10. Then type `python3` to open the Python interpreter.

Shell

```
% python3
Python 3.10.2 (v3.10.2:a58ebcc701, Jan 13 2022, 14:50:16)
 [Clang 13.0.0 (clang-1300.0.29.30)] on darwin
Type "help", "copyright", "credits" or "license" for more information.
>>>
```

Python Interactive Mode

From the command line typing either `python` on Windows or `python3` on macOS will bring up the Python Interpreter, also known as Python Interactive mode. The new prompt of >>> indicates that you are now inside Python itself and **not** the command line. If you try any of the previous shell commands we ran–`cd`, `ls`, `mkdir`–they will each raise errors. What *will* work is actual Python code. For example, try out both `1 + 1` and `print("Hello Python!")` making sure to hit the Enter or Return key after each to run them.

Shell

```
>>> 1 + 1
2
>>> print("Hello Python!")
Hello Python!
```

Python's interactive mode is a great way to save time if you want to try out a short bit of Python code. But it has a number of limitations: you can't save your work in a file and writing longer code snippets is cumbersome. As a result, we will spend most of our time writing Python and Django in files using a text editor.

To exit Python from the command line you can type either `exit()` and the Enter key or use Ctrl + z on Windows or Ctrl + d on macOS.

Virtual Environments

Installing the latest version of Python and Django is the correct approach for any new project. But in the real world, it is common that existing projects rely on older versions of each. Consider the following situation: *Project A* uses Django 2.2 but *Project B* uses Django 4.0? By default, Python and Django are installed *globally* on a computer meaning it is quite a pain to install and reinstall different versions every time you want to switch between projects.

Fortunately, there is a straightforward solution. *Virtual environments* allow you to create and manage separate environments for each Python project on the same computer. There are many areas of software development that are hotly debated, but using virtual environments for Python development is not one. **You should use a dedicated virtual environment for each new Python project**.

There are several ways to implement virtual environments but the simplest is with the venv[7] module already installed as part of the Python 3 standard library. To try it out, navigate to the existing `setup` directory on your Desktop.

Shell

```
# Windows
> cd onedrive\desktop\code\setup

# macOS
% cd ~/desktop/code/setup
```

To create a virtual environment within this new directory use the format `python -m venv <name_-of_env>` on Windows or `python3 -m venv <name_of_env>` on macOS. It is up to the developer to choose a proper environment name but a common choice is to call it `.venv`.

---

[7]https://docs.python.org/3/library/venv.html

Shell

```
# Windows
> python -m venv .venv
> Set-ExecutionPolicy -ExecutionPolicy RemoteSigned -Scope CurrentUser
>

# macOS
% python3 -m venv .venv
(.venv) %
```

If you use the command `ls` to look at our current directory it will appear empty. However the
`.venv` directory is there, it's just that it is "hidden" due to the period `.` that precedes the name.
Hidden files and directories are a way for developers to indicate that the contents are important
and should be treated differently than regular files. To view it, try `ls -la` which shows all
directories and files, even hidden ones.

Shell

```
> ls -la
total 0
drwxr-xr-x  3 wsv   staff    96 Oct  7 11:10 .
drwxr-xr-x  3 wsv   staff    96 Oct  7 11:10 ..
drwxr-xr-x  6 wsv   staff   192 Oct  7 11:10 .venv
```

You will see that `.venv` is there and can be accessed via `cd` if desired. In the directory itself is a
copy of the Python interpreter and a few management scripts, but you will not need to use it
directly in this book.

Once created, a virtual environment must be *activated*. On Windows an *Execution Policy* must
be set to enable running scripts. This is a safety precaution. The Python docs[8] recommend
allowing scripts for the `CurrentUser` only, which is what we will do. On macOS there are no
similar restrictions on scripts so it is possible to directly run `source .venv/bin/activate`.

Here is what the full commands look like to create and activate a new virtual environment called
`.venv`:

---

[8]https://docs.python.org/3/library/venv.html

Shell

```
# Windows
> python -m venv .venv
> Set-ExecutionPolicy -ExecutionPolicy RemoteSigned -Scope CurrentUser
> .venv\Scripts\Activate.ps1
(.venv) >

# macOS
% python3 -m venv .venv
% source .venv/bin/activate
(.venv) %
```

The shell prompt now has the environment name (.venv) prefixed which indicates that the virtual environment is active. Any Python packages installed or updated within this location will be confined to the active virtual environment.

To deactivate and leave a virtual environment type deactivate.

Shell

```
# Windows
(.venv) > deactivate
>

# macOS
(.venv) % deactivate
%
```

The shell prompt no longer has the virtual environment name prefixed which means the session is now back to normal.

Install Django and Django REST Framework

Now that Python is installed and we know how to use virtual environments it is time to install Django and Django REST Framework. In the setup directory reactivate the existing virtual environment.

Shell

```
# Windows
> .venv\Scripts\Activate.ps1
(.venv) >

# macOS
% source .venv/bin/activate
(.venv) %
```

Django is hosted on the Python Package Index (PyPI)[9], a central repository for most Python packages. We will use `pip`, the most popular package installer, which comes included with Python 3. To install the latest version of Django use the command `python -m pip install django~=4.0.0`.

The comparison operator $\sim=$ ensures that subsequent security updates for Django, such as 4.0.1, 4.0.2, and so on are automatically installed. Note that while it is possible to use the shorter version of `pip install <package>`, it is a best practice to use the longer but more explicit form of `python -m pip install <package>` to ensure that the correct version of Python is used. This can be an issue if you have multiple versions of Python installed on your computer.

Shell

```
(.venv) > python -m pip install django~=4.0.0
```

You might see a WARNING message about updating `pip` after running these commands. It's always good to be on the latest version of software and to remove the annoying WARNING message each time you use `pip`. You can either copy and paste the recommended command or run `python -m pip install --upgrade pip` to be on the latest version.

Shell

```
(.venv) > python -m pip install --upgrade pip
```

The latest version of Django REST Framework is 3.12.0. To install it and any future 3.12.x updates use the following command:

---

[9]https://pypi.org

Shell

```
(.venv) > python -m pip install djangorestframework~=3.13.0
```

The command `pip freeze` outputs the contents of your current virtual environment.

Shell

```
(.venv) > pip freeze
asgiref==3.4.1
Django==4.0.0
djangorestframework==3.12.4
pytz==2021.3
sqlparse==0.4.2
```

Ours contains five programs total that have been installed. Django relies on `asgiref`, `pytz`, and `sqlparse` which are automatically added when you install Django.

It is a standard practice to output the contents of a virtual environment to a file called `requirements.txt`. This is a way to keep track of installed packaged and also lets other developers recreate the virtual environment on different computers. Let's do that now by using the `>` operator.

Shell

```
(.venv) > pip freeze > requirements.txt
```

If you look in the `setup` directory there is now an additional file called `requirements.txt`. If you open its contents with your text editor, you'll see it matches the five programs previously outputted to the command line.

Text Editors

The command line is where we execute commands for our programs but a text editor is where actual code is written. The computer doesn't care what text editor you use–the end result is just code–but a good text editor can provide helpful hints and catch typos for you.

There are many modern text editors available but a very popular one is Visual Studio Code[10], which is free, easy to install, and enjoys widespread popularity. If you're not already using a text editor, download and install VSCode from the official website.

An optional–but highly recommended–additional step is to take advance of the large ecosystem of extensions available on VSCode. On Windows, navigate to `File -> Preferences -> Extensions` or on macOS `Code -> Preferences -> Extensions`. This launches a search bar for the extensions marketplace. Enter "python" which will bring up the Microsoft extension as the first result. Install it.

A second extension to add is Black[11], which is a Python code formatter that has quickly become the default within the Python community. To install Black, open a Terminal window within VSCode by going to `Terminal -> New Terminal` at the top of the page. In the new terminal window opened at the bottom of the page, type `python -m pip install black`. Next, open up the VSCode settings by navigating to `File -> Preferences -> Settings` on Windows or `Code -> Preferences -> Settings` on macOS. Search for "python formatting provider" and select `black` from the dropdown options. Then search for "format on save" and enable "Editor: Format on Save". Black will now automatically format your code whenever a `*.py` file is saved.

To confirm this is working, use your text editor to create a new file called `hello.py` within the `setup` directory located on your Desktop and type in the following using single quotes:

hello.py

```
print('Hello, World!')
```

On save, it should be automatically updated to using double quotes which is Black's default preference[12]: `print("Hello, World!")`. That means everything is working properly.

Install Git

The final step is to install *Git*, a version control system that is indispensable to modern software development. With Git you can collaborate with other developers, track all your work via

---

[10]https://code.visualstudio.com/

[11]https://pypi.org/project/black/

[12]https://black.readthedocs.io/en/stable/the_black_code_style/current_style.html#strings

commits, and revert to any previous version of your code even if you accidentally delete something important!

On Windows, navigate to the official website at `https://git-scm.com/` and click on the "Download" link which should install the proper version for your computer. Save the file and then open your Downloads folder and double click on the file. This will launch the Git for Windows installer. Click the "Next" button through most of the early defaults as they are fine and can always be updated later as needed. There are two exceptions however: under "Choosing the default editor used by Git" select VS Code not Vim. And in the section on "Adjusting the name of the initial branch in new repositories" select the option to use "main" as opposed to "master" as the default branch name. Otherwise the recommended defaults are fine and can always be tweaked later if needed.

To confirm Git is installed on Windows, close all current shell windows and then open a new one which will load the changes to our PATH variable. Type in `git --version` which should show it is installed.

Shell

```
# Windows
> git --version
git version 2.33.1.windows.1
```

On macOS, installing Git via Xcode is currently the easiest option. To check if Git is already installed on your computer, type `git --version` in a new terminal window.

Shell

```
# macOS
% git --version
```

If you do not have Git installed, a popup message will ask if you want to install it as part of "command line developer tools." Select "Install" which will load Xcode and its command line tools package. Or if you do not see the message for some reason, type `xcode-select --install` instead to install Xcode directly.

Be aware that Xcode is a very large package so the initial download may take some time. Xcode is primarily designed for building iOS apps but also includes many developer features need on macOS. Once the download is complete close all existing terminal shells, open a new window, and type in `git --version` to confirm the install worked.

Shell

```
# macOS
% git --version
git version 2.30.1 (Apple Git-130)
```

Once Git is installed on your machine we need to do a one-time *system* configuration by declaring the name and email address associated with all your Git commits. We will also set the default branch name to `main`. Within the command line shell type the following two lines. Make sure to update them your name and email address.

Shell

```
> git config --global user.name "Your Name"
> git config --global user.email "yourname@email.com"
> git config --global init.defaultBranch main
```

You can always change these configs later if you desire by retyping the same commands with a new name or email address.

Conclusion

Configuring a new software development environment is no fun at all, even for experienced programmers. But if you've gotten to this point the one-time pain will pay many dividends down the road. We have now learned about the command line, Python interactive mode, and installed the latest version of Python, Django, and Django REST Framework. We installed Git and configured our text editor. Next up we'll learn about web APIs and then dive into creating our own with Django.

Chapter 2: Web APIs

Before we start building our own web APIs with Django it's important to review how the web really works. After all, a "web API" literally sits on top of the existing architecture of the world wide web and relies on a host of technologies including HTTP, TCP/IP, and more.

In this chapter we will review the basic terminology of web APIs: endpoints, resources, HTTP verbs, HTTP status codes, and REST. Even if you already feel comfortable with these terms, I encourage you to read the chapter in full.

World Wide Web

The Internet is a system of interconnected computer networks that has existed since at least the 1960s[13]. However, the internet's early usage was restricted to a small number of isolated networks, largely government, military, or scientific in nature, that exchanged information electronically. By the 1980s, many research institutes and universities were using the internet to share data. In Europe, the biggest internet node was located at CERN (European Organization for Nuclear Research) in Geneva, Switzerland, which operates the largest particle physics laboratory in the world. These experiments generate enormous quantities of data that need to be shared remotely with scientists all around the world.

Compared with today, though, overall internet usage in the 1980s was miniscule. Most people did not have access to it or even understood why it mattered. A small number of internet nodes powered all the traffic and the computers using it were primarily within the same, small networks.

This all changed in 1989 when a research scientist at CERN, Tim Berners-Lee, invented HTTP and ushered in the modern World Wide Web. His great insight was that the existing hypertext[14]

---

[13]https://en.wikipedia.org/wiki/Internet
[14]https://en.wikipedia.org/wiki/Hypertext

system, where text displayed on a computer screen contained links (hyperlinks) to other documents, could be moved onto the internet.

His invention, Hypertext Transfer Protocol (HTTP)[15], was the first standard, universal way to share documents over the internet. It ushered in the concept of web pages: discrete documents with a URL, links, and resources such as images, audio, or video.

Today, when most people think of "the internet," they think of the World Wide Web, which is now the primary way that billions of people and computers communicate online.

URLs

A URL (Uniform Resource Locator) is the address of a resource on the internet. For example, the Google homepage lives at `https://www.google.com`.

When you want to go to the Google homepage, you type the full URL address into a web browser. Your browser then sends a request out over the internet and is magically connected (we'll cover what actually happens shortly) to a server that responds with the data needed to render the Google homepage in your browser.

This **request** and **response** pattern is the basis of all web communication. A **client** (typically a web browser but also a native app or really any internet-connected device) requests information and a **server** responds with a response.

Since web communication occurs via HTTP these are known more formally as HTTP requests and HTTP responses.

Within a given URL are also several discrete components. For example, consider the Google homepage located at `https://www.google.com`. The first part, `https`, refers to the **scheme** used. It tells the web browser *how* to access resources at the location. For a website this is typically `http` or `https`, but it could also be `ftp` for files, `smtp` for email, and so on. The next section, `www.google.com`, is the **hostname** or the actual name of the site. Every URL contains a scheme and a host.

Many webpages also contain an optional **path**, too. If you go to the homepage for Python

---

[15]https://en.wikipedia.org/wiki/Hypertext_Transfer_Protocol

at `https://www.python.org` and click on the link for the "About" page you'll be redirected to `https://www.python.org/about/`. The `/about/` piece is the path.

In summary, every URL like `https://python.org/about/` has three potential parts:

- a scheme - `https`
- a hostname - `www.python.org`
- and an (optional) path - `/about/`

Internet Protocol Suite

Once we know the actual URL of a resource, a whole collection of other technologies must work properly (together) to connect the client with the server and load an actual webpage. This is broadly referred to as the internet protocol suite[16] and there are entire books written on just this topic. For our purposes, however, we can stick to the broad basics.

Several things happen when a user types `https://www.google.com` into their web browser and hits Enter. First the browser needs to find the desired server, somewhere, on the vast internet. It uses a *domain name service* (DNS) to translate the domain name "google.com" into an IP address[17], which is a unique sequence of numbers representing every connected device on the internet. Domain names are used because it is easier for humans to remember a domain name like "google.com" than an IP address like "172.217.164.68".

After the browser has the IP address for a given domain, it needs a way to set up a consistent connection with the desired server. This happens via the *Transmission Control Protocol* (TCP) which provides reliable, ordered, and error-checked delivery of bytes between two application.

To establish a TCP connection between two computers, a three-way "handshake" occurs between the client and server:

1. The client sends a `SYN` asking to establish a connection
2. The server responds with a `SYN-ACK` acknowledging the request and passing a connection parameter

---

[16]https://en.wikipedia.org/wiki/Internet_protocol_suite
[17]https://en.wikipedia.org/wiki/IP_address

3. The client sends an ACK back to the server confirming the connection

Once the TCP connection is established, the two computers can start communicating via HTTP.

HTTP Verbs

Every webpage contains both an address (the URL) as well as a list of approved actions known as HTTP verbs. So far we've mainly talked about getting a web page, but it's also possible to create, edit, and delete content.

Consider the Facebook website. After logging in, you can read your timeline, create a new post, or edit/delete an existing one. These four actions Create-Read-Update-Delete are known colloquially as "CRUD" and represent the overwhelming majority of actions taken online.

The HTTP protocol contains a number of *request methods* that can be used while requesting information from a server. The four most common map to CRUD functionality: POST, GET, PUT, and DELETE.

Diagram

```
CRUD                            HTTP Verbs
----                            ----------
Create   <------------------->  POST
Read     <------------------->  GET
Update   <------------------->  PUT
Delete   <------------------->  DELETE
```

To create content you use POST, to read content GET, to update it PUT, and to delete it you use DELETE.

Endpoints

A traditional website consists of web pages with HTML, CSS, images, JavaScript, and more. There is a dedicated URL, such as example.com/1/, for each page. A web API also relies on URLs and a corresponding one might be example.com/api/1/, but instead of serving up web pages consumable by humans it produces API *endpoints*. An endpoints contains data, typically in the JSON[18] format, and also a list of available actions (HTTP verbs).

For example, we could create the following API endpoints for a new website called `mysite`.

Diagram

```
https://www.mysite.com/api/users         # GET returns all users
https://www.mysite.com/api/users/<id>    # GET returns a single user
```

In the first endpoint, `/api/users`, an available `GET` request returns a list of all available users. This type of endpoint which returns multiple data resources is known as a **collection**.

The second endpoint, `/api/users/<id>`, represents a single user. A `GET` request returns information about just that one user.

If we added a `POST` to the first endpoint we could create a new user, while adding `DELETE` to the second endpoint would allow us to delete a single user.

We will become much more familiar with API endpoints over the course of this book but ultimately creating an API involves making a series of endpoints: URLs that expose JSON data and associated HTTP verbs.

HTTP

We've already talked a lot about HTTP in this chapter, but now we will describe what it actually is and how it works.

HTTP is a *request-response* protocol between two computers that have an existing TCP connection. The computer making the requests is known as the *client* while the computer responding is known as the *server*. Typically a client is a web browser but it could also be an iOS app or really any internet-connected device. A server is a fancy name for any computer optimized to work over the internet. All we really need to transform a basic laptop into a server is some special software and a persistent internet connection.

---

[18]https://json.org/

Every HTTP message consists of a status line, headers, and optional body data. For example, here is a sample HTTP message that a browser might send to request the Google homepage located at `https://www.google.com`.

Diagram

```
GET / HTTP/1.1
Host: google.com
Accept_Language: en-US
```

The top line is known as the *request line* and it specifies the HTTP method to use (`GET`), the path (`/`), and the specific version of HTTP to use (`HTTP/1.1`).

The two subsequent lines are HTTP headers: `Host` is the domain name and `Accept_Language` is the language to use, in this case American English. There are many HTTP headers[19] available.

HTTP messages also have an optional third section, known as the body, however we only see a body message with HTTP responses containing data.

For simplicity, let's assume that the Google homepage only contained the HTML "Hello, World!" This is what the HTTP response message from a Google server might look like.

Diagram

```
HTTP/1.1 200 OK
Date: Mon, 24 Jan 2022 23:26:07 GMT
Server: gws
Accept-Ranges: bytes
Content-Length: 13
Content-Type: text/html; charset=UTF-8

Hello, world!
```

The top line is the *response line* and it specifies that we are using `HTTP/1.1`. The status code `200` `OK` indicates the request by the client was successful (more on status codes shortly).

The next five lines are HTTP headers. And finally, *after a line break*, there is our actual body content of "Hello, world!".

Every HTTP message, whether a request or response, therefore has the following format:

---

[19]https://en.wikipedia.org/wiki/List_of_HTTP_header_fields

Diagram

```
Response/request line
Headers...

(optional) Body
```

Most web pages contain multiple resources that require multiple HTTP request/response cycles. If a webpage had HTML, one CSS file, and an image, three separate trips back-and-forth between the client and server would be required before the complete web page could be rendered in the browser.

Status Codes

Once your web browser has executed an HTTP Request on a URL there is no guarantee things will actually work! Thus there is a quite lengthy list of HTTP Status Codes[20] available to accompany each HTTP response.

You can tell the general *type* of status code based on the following system:

- `2xx Success` - the action requested by the client was received, understood, and accepted
- `3xx Redirection` - the requested URL has moved
- `4xx Client Error` - there was an error, typically a bad URL request by the client
- `5xx Server Error` - the server failed to resolve a request

There is no need to memorize all the available status codes. With practice you will become familiar with the most common ones such as 200 (OK), 201 (Created), 301 (Moved Permanently), 404 (Not Found), and 500 (Server Error).

The important thing to remember is that, generally speaking, there are only four potential outcomes to any given HTTP request: it worked (2xx), it was redirected somehow (3xx), the client made an error (4xx), or the server made an error (5xx).

These status codes are automatically placed in the request/response line at the top of every HTTP message.

---

[20]https://en.wikipedia.org/wiki/List_of_HTTP_status_codes

Statelessness

A final important point to make about HTTP is that it is a **stateless** protocol. This means each request/response pair is completely independent of the previous one. There is no stored memory of past interactions, which is known as state[21] in computer science.

Statelessness brings a lot of benefits to HTTP. Since all electronic communication systems have signal loss over time, if we *did not* have a stateless protocol, things would constantly break if one request/response cycle didn't go through. As a result, HTTP is known as a very resilient distributed protocol.

The downside is that managing state is really, really important in web applications. State is how a website remembers that you've logged in and how an e-commerce site manages your shopping cart. It's fundamental to how we use modern websites, yet it's not supported on HTTP itself.

Historically, state was maintained on the server but it has moved more and more to the client, the web browser, in modern front-end frameworks like React, Angular, and Vue. We'll learn more about state when we cover user authentication but remember that HTTP is stateless. This makes it very good for reliably sending information between two computers, but bad at remembering anything outside of each individual request/response pair.

REST

REpresentational State Transfer (REST)[22] is an architecture first proposed in 2000 by Roy Fielding in his dissertation thesis. It is an approach to building APIs on top of the web, which means on top of the HTTP protocol.

Entire books have been written on what makes an API actually RESTful or not. But there are three main traits that we will focus on here for our purposes. Every RESTful API:

- is stateless, like HTTP
- supports common HTTP verbs (GET, POST, PUT, DELETE, etc.)

---

[21]https://en.wikipedia.org/wiki/State_(computer_science)
[22]https://en.wikipedia.org/wiki/Representational_state_transfer

- returns data in either the JSON or XML format

Any RESTful API must, at a minimum, have these three principles. The standard is important because it provides a consistent way to both design and consume web APIs.

Conclusion

While there is **a lot** of technology underlying the modern world wide web, we as developers don't have to implement it all from scratch. The beautiful combination of Django and Django REST Framework handles, properly, most of the complexity involved with web APIs. However, it is important to have at least a broad understanding of how all the pieces fit together.

Ultimately, a web API is a collection of endpoints that expose certain parts of an underlying database. As developers we control the URLs for each endpoint, what underlying data is available, and what actions are possible via HTTP verbs. By using HTTP headers we can set various levels of authentication and permission too as we will see later in the book.

Chapter 3: Library Website

Django REST Framework works alongside the Django web framework to create web APIs. We cannot build a web API with only Django Rest Framework. It always must be added to a project *after* Django itself has been installed and configured.

In this chapter, we will review the similarities and differences between traditional Django and Django REST Framework. The most important takeaway is that Django creates websites containing webpages, while Django REST Framework creates web APIs which are a collection of URL endpoints containing available HTTP verbs that return JSON.

To illustrate these concepts, we will build out a basic *Library* website with traditional Django and then extend it into a web API with Django REST Framework.

Traditional Django

Navigate to the existing `code` directory on the Desktop and make sure you are not in a current virtual environment. You should *not* see (.venv) before the shell prompt. If you do, use the command `deactivate` to leave it. Make a new directory called `library`, create a new virtual environment, activate it, and install Django.

Shell

```
# Windows
> cd onedrive\desktop\code
> mkdir library
> cd library
> python -m venv .venv
> .venv\Scripts\Activate.ps1
(.venv) > python -m pip install django~=4.0.0

# macOS
% cd desktop/desktop/code
% mkdir library
% cd library
```

```
% python3 -m venv .venv
% source .venv/bin/activate
(.venv) % python3 -m pip install django~=4.0.0
```

A traditional Django website consists of a single *project* with multiple *apps* representing discrete functionality. Let's create a new project with the `startproject` command called `django_project`. Don't forget to include the period . at the end which installs the code in our current directory. If you do not include the period, Django will create an additional directory by default.

Shell

```
(.venv) > django-admin startproject django_project .
```

Pause for a moment to examine the default project structure Django has provided for us. You examine this visually if you like by opening the new directory with your mouse on the Desktop. The `.venv` directory may not be initially visible because it is "hidden" but nonetheless still there.

Code

```
├── django_project
│   ├── __init__.py
│   ├── asgi.py
│   ├── settings.py
│   ├── urls.py
│   └── wsgi.py
├── manage.py
└── .venv/
```

The `.venv` directory was created with our virtual environment but Django has added a `django_-project` directory and a `manage.py` file. Within `django_project` are five new files:

- `__init__.py` indicates that the files in the folder are part of a Python package. Without this file, we cannot import files from another directory which we will be doing a lot of in Django!
- `asgi.py` allows for an optional Asynchronous Server Gateway Interface[23] to be run
- `settings.py` controls our Django project's overall settings

---

[23]https://asgi.readthedocs.io/en/latest/specs/main.html

- `urls.py` tells Django which pages to build in response to a browser or URL request
- `wsgi.py` stands for Web Server Gateway Interface[24] which helps Django serve our eventual web pages.

The `manage.py` file is not part of `django_project` but is used to execute various Django commands such as running the local web server or creating a new app. Let's use it now with `migrate` to sync the database with Django's default settings and start up the local Django web server with `runserver`.

Shell

```
(.venv) > python manage.py migrate
(.venv) > python manage.py runserver
```

Open a web browser to http://127.0.0.1:8000/[25] to confirm our project is successfully installed and running.

---

[24]https://en.wikipedia.org/wiki/Web_Server_Gateway_Interface
[25]http://127.0.0.1:8000/

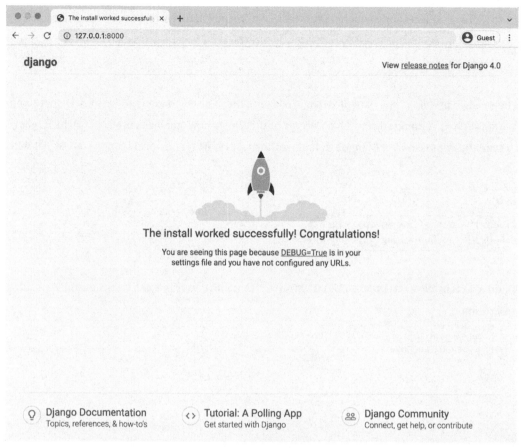

Django welcome page

First app

The next step is to add our first app which we'll call `books`. Stop the local server by typing `Control+c` and then run the `startapp` command plus our app name to create it.

Shell

```
(.venv) > python manage.py startapp books
```

Now let's explore the app files Django has automatically created for us.

Shell

```
├── books
│   ├── __init__.py
│   ├── admin.py
│   ├── apps.py
│   ├── migrations
│   │   └── __init__.py
│   ├── models.py
│   ├── tests.py
│   └── views.py
```

Each app has a `__init__.py` file identifying it as a Python package and there are 6 new files created:

- `admin.py` is a configuration file for the built-in Django Admin app
- `apps.py` is a configuration file for the app itself
- `migrations/` is a directory that stores migrations files for database changes
- `models.py` is where we define our database models
- `tests.py` is for our app-specific tests
- `views.py` is where we handle the request/response logic for our web app

Typically, developers will also create an `urls.py` file within each app for routing. We'll do that shortly.

Before moving on we must add our new app to the `INSTALLED_APPS` configuration in the `django_-project/settings.py`. Do so now with your text editor.

Code

```
# django_project/settings.py
INSTALLED_APPS = [
    "django.contrib.admin",
    "django.contrib.auth",
    "django.contrib.contenttypes",
    "django.contrib.sessions",
    "django.contrib.messages",
    "django.contrib.staticfiles",
    # Local
    "books.apps.BooksConfig",  # new
]
```

Each web page in traditional Django requires several files: `views.py`, `urls.py`, template, and `models.py`. Let's start with the database model to structure our Library data.

Models

In your text editor, open up the file `books/models.py` and update it as follows:

Code

```
# books/models.py
from django.db import models


class Book(models.Model):
    title = models.CharField(max_length=250)
    subtitle = models.CharField(max_length=250)
    author = models.CharField(max_length=100)
    isbn = models.CharField(max_length=13)

    def __str__(self):
        return self.title
```

This is a basic Django model where `models` is imported from Django on the top line and a new class, called `Book`, extends it. There are four fields: `title`, `subtitle`, `author`, and `isbn`. We also include a `__str__` method so that the title of a book will display in readable format in the admin later on. Note that an ISBN is a unique, 13-character identifier assigned to every published book.

Since we created a new database model we need to create a migration file to go along with it. Specifying the app name is optional but recommended. We *could* just type `python manage.py makemigrations` but if there were multiple apps with database changes, both would be added to the migrations file which makes debugging in the future more of a challenge. Keep your migrations files as specific as possible.

Shell

```
(.venv) > python manage.py makemigrations books
Migrations for 'books':
  books/migrations/0001_initial.py
    - Create model Book
```

Then second step after creating a migrations file is to `migrate` it so it is applied to the existing database.

Shell

```
(.venv) > python manage.py migrate
Operations to perform:
  Apply all migrations: admin, auth, books, contenttypes, sessions
Running migrations:
  Applying books.0001_initial... OK
```

So far so good. If any of this feels brand new to you I suggest taking a pause to review Django for Beginners[26] for a more-detailed explanation of traditional Django projects.

Admin

We can start entering data into our new model via the built-in Django app. To use it we need to create a superuser account and update the `books/admin.py` file so the `books` app is displayed.

Start with the superuser account. On the command line run the following command:

---

[26]https://djangoforbeginners.com/

Shell

```
(.venv) > python manage.py createsuperuser
```

Follow the prompts to enter a username, email, and password. Note that for security reasons, text will not appear on the screen while entering your password.

Now update our `books` app's `admin.py` file.

Code

```
# books/admin.py
from django.contrib import admin

from .models import Book

admin.site.register(Book)
```

That's all we need! Start up the local server again.

Shell

```
(.venv) > python manage.py runserver
```

Navigate to `http://127.0.0.1:8000/admin` and log in. This brings up the admin homepage.

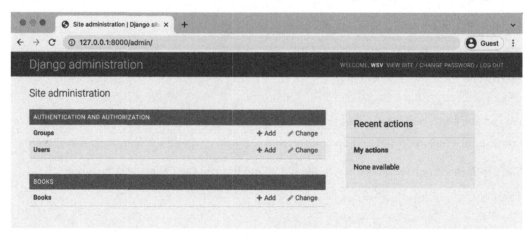

Admin homepage

Click on the "+ Add" link next to Books.

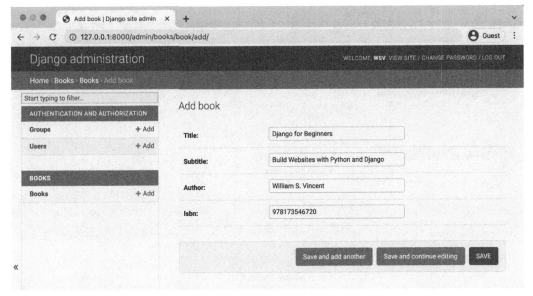

Admin add book

I've entered in the details for my three books: Django for Beginners, Django for APIs, and Django for Professionals. After clicking the "Save" button we are redirected to the "Books" page that lists all current entries.

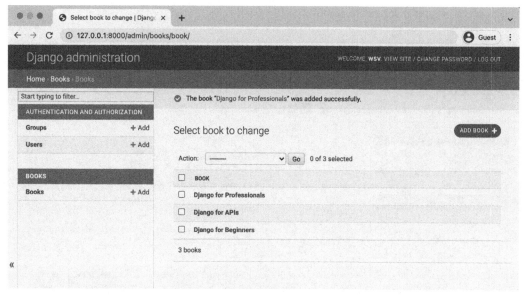

Admin books list

Our traditional Django project has data now but we need a way to expose it as a web page. That means creating views, URLs, and template files. Let's do that now.

Views

The `views.py` file controls *how* the database model content is displayed. Since we want to list all books we can use the built-in generic class ListView[27]. Update the `books/views.py` file.

---

[27]https://docs.djangoproject.com/en/4.0/ref/class-based-views/generic-display/#django.views.generic.list. ListView

Code

```
# books/views.py
from django.views.generic import ListView

from .models import Book


class BookListView(ListView):
    model = Book
    template_name = "book_list.html"
```

On the top lines we import `ListView` and our `Book` model. Then we create a `BookListView` class that specifies the model to use and the not-yet-created template.

Two more steps before we have a working web page: create our template and configure our URLs. Let's start with the URLs.

URLs

We need to set up both the project-level `urls.py` file and then one within the `books` app. When a user visits our site they will initially interact with the `django_project/urls.py` file so let's configure that one first. Add the `include` import on the second line and then a new path for the `books` app.

Code

```
# django_project/urls.py
from django.contrib import admin
from django.urls import path, include  # new

urlpatterns = [
    path("admin/", admin.site.urls),
    path("", include("books.urls")),  # new
]
```

The top two lines import the built-in `admin` app, `path` for our routes, and `include` which will be used with our `books` app. We use the empty string, `""`, for the `books` app route which means a user on the homepage will be redirected directly to the `books` app.

Now we can configure our books/urls.py file. But, oops! Django for some reason does not include a urls.py file by default in apps so we need to create it ourself. In your text editor create a new file called books/urls.py and update it as follows:

Code

```
# books/urls.py
from django.urls import path

from .views import BookListView

urlpatterns = [
    path("", BookListView.as_view(), name="home"),
]
```

We import our views file, configure BookListView at the empty string, "", and add a named URL[28], home, as a best practice.

Now when a user goes to the homepage of our website they will first hit the django_project/urls.py file, then be redirected to books/urls.py which specifies using the BookListView. In this view file, the Book model is used along with ListView to list out all books.

Templates

The final step is to create our template file that controls the layout on the actual web page. We have already specified its name as book_list.html in our view. There are two options for its location: by default the Django template loader will look for templates within our books app in the following location: books/templates/books/book_list.html. We could also create a separate, project-level templates directory instead and update our django_project/settings.py file to point there.

Which one you ultimately use in your own projects is a personal preference. We will use the default structure here.

Start by making a new templates folder within the books app and within it a books folder. This can be done from the terminal shell. If it is still running the local server use the command Control+c to stop it.

---

[28]https://docs.djangoproject.com/en/4.0/topics/http/urls/#naming-url-patterns

Shell

```
(.venv) > mkdir books/templates
(.venv) > mkdir books/templates/books
```

With your text editor create a new file called `books/templates/books/book_list.html`. It will contain the following code:

HTML

```
<!-- books/templates/books/book_list.html -->
<h1>All books</h1>
{% for book in book_list %}
<ul>
  <li>Title: {{ book.title }}</li>
  <li>Subtitle: {{ book.subtitle }}</li>
  <li>Author: {{ book.author }}</li>
  <li>ISBN: {{ book.isbn }}</li>
</ul>
{% endfor %}
```

Django ships with a template language[29] that allows for basic logic. Here we use the for[30] tag to loop over all available books. Template tags must be included within opening/closing brackets and parentheses. So the format is always {% for ... %} and then we must close our loop later with {% endfor %}.

What we are looping over is the object containing all available books in our model courtesy of `ListView`. The name of this object is `<model>_list` which, given our model is named `book`, means it is `book_list`. Therefore to loop over each book we write {% for book in book_list %}. And then display each field from our model.

Now we can start up the local Django server again.

---

[29] https://docs.djangoproject.com/en/4.0/ref/templates/language/
[30] https://docs.djangoproject.com/en/4.0/ref/templates/builtins/#std:templatetag-for

Shell

```
(.venv) > python manage.py runserver
```

Navigate to the homepage at `http://127.0.0.1:8000/` to see our work.

Book web page

If we add additional books in the admin, they will each appear here, too.

Tests

Tests are a vital part of writing software and we should add them now before moving on to the API portion of this project. We want to be sure that the Book model works as expected as well as our view, urls, and template. Our books app already has an empty `books/tests.py` file that we can use for this.

Code

```python
# books/tests.py
from django.test import TestCase
from django.urls import reverse

from .models import Book


class BookTests(TestCase):
    @classmethod
    def setUpTestData(cls):
        cls.book = Book.objects.create(
            title="A good title",
            subtitle="An excellent subtitle",
            author="Tom Christie",
            isbn="1234567890123",
        )

    def test_book_content(self):
        self.assertEqual(self.book.title, "A good title")
        self.assertEqual(self.book.subtitle, "An excellent subtitle")
        self.assertEqual(self.book.author, "Tom Christie")
        self.assertEqual(self.book.isbn, "1234567890123")

    def test_book_listview(self):
        response = self.client.get(reverse("home"))
        self.assertEqual(response.status_code, 200)
        self.assertContains(response, "excellent subtitle")
        self.assertTemplateUsed(response, "books/book_list.html")
```

At the top of the file we import Django's TestCase class, reverse so we can confirm the named URL used, and our single model Book.

Then we create a class called BookTests and fill setUpTestData with dummy information for a book. All tests must start with the name test_ in order to be run by Django so we create one to test the book's content, test_book_content, that performs an assertEqual on each field. Next we test our listview with test_book_listview that checks the response uses the named URL "home", it returns an HTTP Status Code of 200, contains the expected text, and uses our template at books/book_list.html.

Make sure the local server is not running and then use the shell command python manage.py test to execute the tests.

Shell

```
(.venv) > python manage.py test
Creating test database for alias 'default'...
System check identified no issues (0 silenced).
..
-------------------------------------------------------------------
Ran 2 tests in 0.007s

OK
Destroying test database for alias 'default'...
```

They all pass! Great, we can move on with our project.

Git

Whenever we have added new code it is a good idea to track our progress using Git. Make sure you've stopped the local server with Control+c. Then run git init to initialize a new repo and git status to check its contents.

Shell

```
(.venv) > git init
(.venv) > git status
On branch main

No commits yet

Untracked files:
  (use "git add <file>..." to include in what will be committed)
        .venv/
        books/
        db.sqlite3
        django_project/
        manage.py

nothing added to commit but untracked files present (use "git add" to track)
```

At the moment, the virtual environment `.venv` is included which is *not* a best practice because it can contain secret information such as API keys that we do not want to be tracked. To fix this create a new file with your text editor called `.gitignore` in the project-level directory next to `manage.py`. A `.gitignore` file tells Git what to ignore. Add a single line for `.venv`.

.gitignore

```
.venv/
```

If you run `git status` again you will see that `.venv` is not longer there. It has been "ignored" by Git. We do, however, want a record of all packages installed in the virtual environment. The current best practice is to run the command `pip freeze` with the > operator to output the contents to a new file called `requirements.txt`.

Shell

```
(.venv) > pip freeze > requirements.txt
```

Let's add *all* our work by using the command `add -A` and then `commit` the changes along with a message (`-m`) describing what has changed.

Shell

```
(.venv) > git add -A
(.venv) > git commit -m "initial commit"
```

Conclusion

This chapter has been all about setting up a traditional Django project. We went through the standard steps of creating a new project, adding a new app, and then updating models, views, urls, and templates. The `admin.py` file has to be updated so we can see our new content and we added tests to ensure our code works and we can add new functionality without worrying about a mistake.

In the next chapter we'll add Django REST Framework and see how quickly a traditional Django website can be transformed into a web API.

Chapter 4: Library API

Our Library website currently consists of a single page that displays all books in the database. To transform it into a web API we will install Django REST Framework and create a new URL that acts an API endpoint outputting all available books. If you recall from Chapter 2, a web API does not output a traditional webpage with HTML, CSS, and JavaScript. Instead, it is just pure data (often in the JSON format) and accompanying HTTP verbs that specify what user actions are allowed. In this instance, an API user can only *read* the content, they are not able to update it in any way though we will learn how to do that in future chapters.

Django REST Framework

As we saw in Chapter 1, adding Django REST Framework is just like installing any other third-party app. Make sure to quit the local server with Control+c if it is still running. Then on the command line type the following.

Shell

```
(.venv) > python -m pip install djangorestframework~=3.13.0
```

We have to formally notify Django of the new installation in our django_project/settings.py file. Scroll down to the INSTALLED_APPS section and add rest_framework. I like to make a distinction between third-party apps and local apps since the number of apps grows quickly in most projects.

Code

```
# django_project/settings.py
INSTALLED_APPS = [
    "django.contrib.admin",
    "django.contrib.auth",
    "django.contrib.contenttypes",
    "django.contrib.sessions",
    "django.contrib.messages",
    "django.contrib.staticfiles",
    # 3rd party
    "rest_framework",  # new
    # Local
    "books.apps.BooksConfig",
]
```

Ultimately, our web API will expose a single endpoint that lists out all books in JSON. To do this, we will need a new URL route, a new view, and a new serializer file (more on this shortly).

There are multiple ways to organize these files. Many professional Django developers will just include API logic in the related app while putting URLs under an /api/ prefix. For now though, to keep the API logic clear from the traditional Django logic, we will create a dedicated apis app for our project.

Let's do that now by using the startapp command. Remember that apps should always have a plural name since Django will otherwise automatically add an s is the admin and other locations.

Shell

```
(.venv) > python manage.py startapp apis
```

Then add it to INSTALLED_APPS in our "Local" section.

Code

```
# django_project/settings.py
INSTALLED_APPS = [
    "django.contrib.admin",
    "django.contrib.auth",
    "django.contrib.contenttypes",
    "django.contrib.sessions",
    "django.contrib.messages",
    "django.contrib.staticfiles",
    # 3rd party
    "rest_framework",
    # Local
    "books.apps.BooksConfig",
    "apis.apps.ApisConfig",  # new
]
```

The apis app will not have its own database models so there is no need to create a migration file and run migrate to update the database. In fact, the database models are the one area we don't need to touch at all since this new web API is designed to expose existing data not create new data.

URLs

Let's start with our URL configs. Adding an API endpoint is just like configuring a traditional Django URL route. In the project-level django_project/urls.py file include the apis app and configure its URL route, which will be at api/.

Code

```
# django_project/urls.py
from django.contrib import admin
from django.urls import path, include

urlpatterns = [
    path("admin/", admin.site.urls),
    path("api/", include("apis.urls")),  # new
    path("", include("books.urls")),
]
```

Then create a new file called apis/urls.py with your text editor. This file will import a future view called BookAPIView and set it to the URL route of "" so it will appear at api/. As always, we'll add a name to it as well, book_list, which helps in the future when we want to refer to this specific route.

Code

```
# apis/urls.py
from django.urls import path

from .views import BookAPIView

urlpatterns = [
    path("", BookAPIView.as_view(), name="book_list"),
]
```

All set.

Views

In traditional Django *views* are used to customize what data to send to the templates. Django REST Framework views are similar except the end result is serialized data in JSON format, not the content for a web page! Django REST Framework views rely on a model, a URL, and a new file called a serializer that we'll see in the next section.

There are generic Django REST Framework views for common use cases and we'll use ListAPIView[31] here to display all books.

---

[31]http://www.django-rest-framework.org/api-guide/generic-views/#listapiview

To avoid confusion, some developers will call an API views file `apiviews.py` or `api.py`. Personally, when working within a dedicated `apis` app I do not find it confusing to just call a Django REST Framework views file `views.py` but opinion varies on this point.

Update the `apis/views.py` file so it looks like the following:

Code

```
# apis/views.py
from rest_framework import generics

from books.models import Book
from .serializers import BookSerializer


class BookAPIView(generics.ListAPIView):
    queryset = Book.objects.all()
    serializer_class = BookSerializer
```

On the top lines we have imported Django REST Framework's generics[32] class of views, the `Book` model from our `books` app, and `serializers` from our `api` app. We will create the serializer used here, `BookSerializer`, in the following section.

Then we create a view class called `BookAPIView` that uses `ListAPIView` to create a read-only endpoint for all book instances. There are many generic views available and we will explore them further in later chapters.

The only two steps required in our view are to specify the `queryset`, which is all available books, and then the `serializer_class` which will be `BookSerializer`.

Serializers

We're on the final step now! So far we have created a `urls.py` file and a `views.py` file for our API. The last–but most important–action is to create our serializer.

A serializer[33] translates complex data like querysets and model instances into a format that is easy to consume over the internet, typically JSON. It is also possible to "deserialize" data, literally

---

[32]https://www.django-rest-framework.org/api-guide/generic-views/#generic-views
[33]https://www.django-rest-framework.org/api-guide/serializers/

the same process in reverse, whereby JSON data is first validated and then transformed into a dictionary.

The real beauty of Django REST Framework lies in its serializers which abstracts away most of the complexity for us. We will cover serialization and JSON in more depth in future chapters but for now the goal is to demonstrate how easy it is to create a serializer with Django REST Framework.

In your text editor, create a new file called `apis/serializers.py` and update it as follows:

Code

```
# apis/serializers.py
from rest_framework import serializers

from books.models import Book


class BookSerializer(serializers.ModelSerializer):
    class Meta:
        model = Book
        fields = ("title", "subtitle", "author", "isbn")
```

On the top lines we import Django REST Framework's `serializers` class and the `Book` model from our `books` app. Next, we extend Django REST Framework's ModelSerializer[34] into a `BookSerializer` class that specifies our database model, `Book`, and the database fields we want to expose of `title`, `subtitle`, `author`, and `isbn`.

And that's it! We're done. By creating a new URL route, a new view, and a serializer class we have created an API endpoint for our Library website that will display all existing books in list format.

Browsable API

Raw JSON data is not particularly friendly to consume with human eyes. Fortunately, Django REST Framework ships with a built-in browsable API that displays both the content and HTTP verbs associated with a given endpoint. To see it in action start up the local web server with the `runserver` command.

---

[34]https://www.django-rest-framework.org/api-guide/serializers/#modelserializer

Shell

```
(.venv) > python manage.py runserver
```

We know the location of our API endpoint is at `http://127.0.0.1:8000/api/` so navigate there in your web browser.

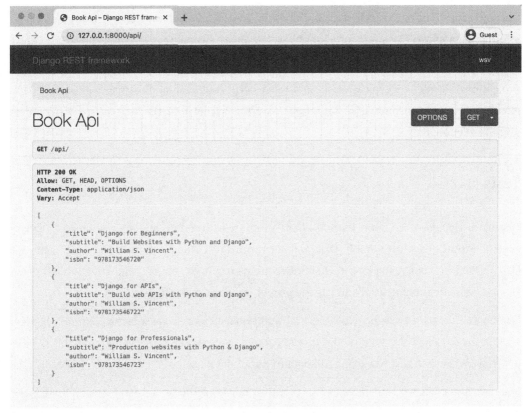

Book API

And look at that! Django REST Framework provides this visualization by default. It displays the HTTP status code for the page, which is `200` meaning `OK`. Specifies `Content-Type` is JSON. And displays the information for our single book entry in a formatted manner.

If you click on the "Get" button in the upper right corner and select "json" at the top of the dropdown list you'll see what the raw API endpoint looks like.

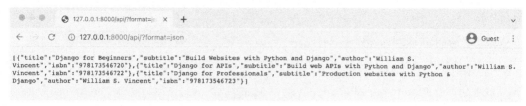

[{"title":"Django for Beginners","subtitle":"Build Websites with Python and Django","author":"William S. Vincent","isbn":"978173546720"},{"title":"Django for APIs","subtitle":"Build web APIs with Python and Django","author":"William S. Vincent","isbn":"978173546722"},{"title":"Django for Professionals","subtitle":"Production websites with Python & Django","author":"William S. Vincent","isbn":"978173546723"}]

Book API JSON

Not very appealing is it? The data is not formatted at all and we can't see any additional information about HTTP status or allowable verbs either. I think we can agree the Django REST Framework version is more appealing.

Professional developers typically use on a third-party tool such as Postman[35] or, if on a Mac, Paw[36], to test and consume APIs. But for our purposes in this book the built-in browsable API is more than enough.

Tests

Testing in Django relies upon Python's built-in unittest[37] module and several helpful Django-specific extensions. Most notably, Django comes with a test client[38] that we can use to simulate GET or POST requests, check the chain of redirects in a web request, and check that a given Django template is being used and has the proper template context data.

Django REST Framework provides several additional helper classes[39] that extend Django's existing test framework. One of these is `APIClient`, an extension of Django's default `Client`, which we will use to test retrieving API data from our database.

Since we already have tests in `books/tests.py` for our Book model we can focus on testing the API endpoint, specifically that it uses the URL we expect, has the correct status code of 200, and contains the correct content.

Open the `apis/tests.py` file with your text editor and fill in the following code which we will review below.

---

[35]https://www.postman.com/

[36]https://paw.cloud/

[37]https://docs.python.org/3/library/unittest.html#module-unittest

[38]https://docs.djangoproject.com/en/4.0/topics/testing/tools/#the-test-client

[39]https://www.django-rest-framework.org/api-guide/testing/

Code

```python
# apis/tests.py
from django.urls import reverse
from rest_framework import status
from rest_framework.test import APITestCase

from books.models import Book


class APITests(APITestCase):
    @classmethod
    def setUpTestData(cls):
        cls.book = Book.objects.create(
            title="Django for APIs",
            subtitle="Build web APIs with Python and Django",
            author="William S. Vincent",
            isbn="9781735467221",
        )

    def test_api_listview(self):
        response = self.client.get(reverse("book_list"))
        self.assertEqual(response.status_code, status.HTTP_200_OK)
        self.assertEqual(Book.objects.count(), 1)
        self.assertContains(response, self.book)
```

At the top we import `reverse` from Django and from Django REST Framework both `status` and `APITestCase`. We also import our Book model though note that since we are in the `api` app we must specify the app name of `book` to import it.

We extend `APITestCase` in a new class called `APITests` that starts by configuring set up data. Then we run four different checks. First we check that the named URL of "book_list" is being used. Second we confirm that HTTP status code matches 200. Third we check that there is a single entry in the database. And finally we confirm that the response contains all the data from our created book object.

Make sure to stop the local server and run the test to confirm that it passes.

Shell

```
(.venv) > python manage.py test
Creating test database for alias 'default'...
System check identified no issues (0 silenced).
...
----------------------------------------------------------------------
Ran 3 tests in 0.009s

OK
Destroying test database for alias 'default'...
```

Note that the output describes three tests passing because we had two in books/tests.py and one here. In larger websites with hundreds or even thousands of tests, performance can become an issue and sometimes you want to check just test within a given app before running the full website test suite. To do that, simply add the name of the app you wish to check to the end of python manage.py test.

Shell

```
(.venv) > python manage.py test apis
Creating test database for alias 'default'...
System check identified no issues (0 silenced).
.
----------------------------------------------------------------------
Ran 1 test in 0.005s

OK
Destroying test database for alias 'default'...
```

Deployment

Deploying a web API is almost identical to deploying a traditional website. We will use Heroku in this book as it provides a free tier and is a widely used Platform-As-a-Service that removes much of the complexity inherent in deployment.

If this is your first time using Heroku, you can sign up for a free account on their website[40]. After completing the registration form wait for the verification email to confirm your account. It will

---

[40]https://www.heroku.com/

take you to the password setup page and, once configured, you will be directed to the dashboard section of Heroku's site. Heroku now also requires enrolling in multi-factor authentication (MFA), which can be done with SalesForce or a tool like Google Authenticator.

We will be using Heroku's *Command Line Interface (CLI)* so we can deploy from the command line. Currently, we are operating within a virtual environment for our *Library* project but we want Heroku available globally, that is everywhere on our machine. An easy way to do so is open up a new command line tab–`Control+t` on Windows, `Command+t` on a Mac–which is not operating in a virtual environment. Anything installed here will be global.

On Windows, see the Heroku CLI page[41] to correctly install either the 32-bit or 64-bit version. On a Mac, the package manager Homebrew[42] is used for installation. If not already on your machine, install Homebrew by copy and pasting the long command on the Homebrew website into your command line and hitting `Return`. It will look something like this:

Shell

```
% /bin/bash -c "$(curl -fsSL https://raw.githubusercontent.com/Homebrew/\
   install/HEAD/install.sh)"
```

Next install the Heroku CLI by copy and pasting the following into your command line and hitting `Return`.

Shell

```
% brew tap heroku/brew && brew install heroku
```

If you are on a new M1 chip Apple computer you might receive an error with something like `Bad CPU type in executable`. Installing Rosetta 2[43] will solve the issue.

Once installation is complete you can close the new command line tab and return to the initial tab with the `pages` virtual environment active.

To verify the installation worked properly run `heroku --version`. There should be output with the current version of the Heroku CLI installed.

---

[41]https://devcenter.heroku.com/articles/heroku-cli#download-and-install
[42]https://brew.sh/
[43]https://support.apple.com/en-us/HT211861

Shell

```
(.venv) > heroku --version
heroku/7.59.2 darwin-x64 node-v12.21.0
```

If you see an error message here on VSCode for Windows about "the term 'heroku' is not recognized..." it is likely a permissions issue. Try opening up the PowerShell app directly and executing `heroku --version`. It should work properly. The VSCode Terminal Shell has some subtle issues from time to time unfortunately.

And if you receive a "Warning" that your Heroku version is out of date try running `heroku update` to install the latest version.

Once you have seen the installed version of Heroku, type the command `heroku login` and use the email and password for Heroku you just set.

Shell

```
(.venv) > heroku login
Enter your Heroku credentials:
Email: will@wsvincent.com
Password: *******************************
Logged in as will@wsvincent.com
```

You might need to verify your credentials on the Heroku website but once the terminal shell confirms your log in you are ready to proceed.

Static Files

Static files[44] are somewhat tricky to deploy properly on Django projects but the good news is that the process for Django APIs is essentially the same. Even though we do not have any of our own at this point, there are static files included in the Django admin and Django REST Framework browsable API so in order for those to deploy properly we must configure all static files.

First we need to create a dedicated `static` directory.

---

[44]https://docs.djangoproject.com/en/4.0/howto/static-files/

Shell

```
(.venv) > mkdir static
```

Git will not track empty directories so it's important to add a .keep file so the static directory is included in source control. Do so now with your text editor.

Then we'll install the WhiteNoise[45] package since Django does not support serving static files in production itself.

Shell

```
(.venv) > python -m pip install whitenoise==6.0.0
```

WhiteNoise must be added to django_project/settings.py in the following locations:

- whitenoise above django.contrib.staticfiles in INSTALLED_APPS
- WhiteNoiseMiddleware above CommonMiddleware
- STATICFILES_STORAGE configuration pointing to WhiteNoise

Code

```
# django_project/settings.py
INSTALLED_APPS = [
    ...
    "whitenoise.runserver_nostatic",  # new
    "django.contrib.staticfiles",
]

MIDDLEWARE = [
    "django.middleware.security.SecurityMiddleware",
    "django.contrib.sessions.middleware.SessionMiddleware",
    "whitenoise.middleware.WhiteNoiseMiddleware",  # new
    ...
]

STATIC_URL = "/static/"
STATICFILES_DIRS = [str(BASE_DIR.joinpath("static"))]  # new
STATIC_ROOT = str(BASE_DIR.joinpath("staticfiles"))  # new
STATICFILES_STORAGE =
    "whitenoise.storage.CompressedManifestStaticFilesStorage"  # new
```

---

[45]http://whitenoise.evans.io/en/stable/

The last step is to run the `collectstatic` command for the first time to compile all the static file directories and files into one self-contained unit suitable for deployment.

Shell

```
(.venv) > python manage.py collectstatic
```

All set. Now that our static files are properly configured we don't have to think much about them going forward!

Deployment Checklist

For a basic deployment we have five items on our deployment checklist:

- install Gunicorn[46] as the production web server
- create a `requirements.txt` file
- create a `runtime.txt` file
- update the `ALLOWED_HOSTS` configuration
- create a `Procfile` for Heroku

Django's built-in web server is fine for local testing but either Gunicorn or uWSGI[47] should be used in production. Since Gunicorn is the simpler of the two to use, it will be our choice. Install it via Pip.

Shell

```
(.venv) > python -m pip install gunicorn~=20.1.0
```

In the previous chapter we created a `requirements.txt` file but we have since installed Django REST Framework and Gunicorn in our virtual environment. Neither is reflected in the current file. It is simple enough though to simply run the command again with the > operator to update it.

---

[46]https://gunicorn.org/
[47]https://uwsgi-docs.readthedocs.io/en/latest/

Shell

```
(.venv) > python -m pip freeze > requirements.txt
```

The third step is to create a `runtime.txt` file in the root directory, next to `requirements.txt`, that specifies what version of Python to run on Heroku. If not set explicitly this is currently set[48] to the `python-3.9.10` runtime but changes over time.

Since we are using Python 3.10 we must create a dedicated runtime.txt[49] file to use it. In your text editor, create this new `runtime.txt` file at the project-level meaning it is in the same directory as the `manage.py` file. As of this writing, the latest version is `3.10.2`. Make sure everything is lowercased!

runtime.txt

```
python-3.10.2
```

The fourth step is to update `ALLOWED_HOSTS`. By default it is set to accept all hosts but we want to restrict access on a live website and API. We want to be able to use either `localhost` or `127.0.0.1` locally and we also know that any Heroku site will end with `.herokuapp.com`. Add all three hosts to our `ALLOWED_HOSTS` configuration.

Code

```
# django_project/settings.py
ALLOWED_HOSTS = [".herokuapp.com", "localhost", "127.0.0.1"]
```

And the final step in your text editor is to create a new `Procfile` in the project root directory next to the `manage.py` file. This is a file specifically for Heroku that provides instructions for running our website. We're telling it to use Gunicorn as the webserver, look for the WSGI configuration in `django_project.wsgi`, and also to output log files which is an optional but helpful additional config.

---

[48]https://devcenter.heroku.com/articles/python-support#specifying-a-python-version
[49]https://devcenter.heroku.com/articles/python-runtimes

Procfile

```
web: gunicorn django_project.wsgi --log-file -
```

We're all set. Add and commit our new changes to Git.

Shell

```
(.venv) > git status
(.venv) > git add -A
(.venv) > git commit -m "New updates for Heroku deployment"
```

GitHub

It is recommended to also store your code on a hosting provider like GitHub, GitLab, or BitBucket. GitHub is very popular and provides a generous free tier so we will use it in this book. You can create a free account on the website.

Once setup, create a new repo[50] called library and make sure to select the "Private" radio button. Then click on the "Create repository" button. On the next page, scroll down to where it says "...or push an existing repository from the command line." Copy and paste the two commands there into your terminal.

It should look like the below albeit instead of wsvincent as the username it will be your GitHub username.

Shell

```
(.venv) > git remote add origin https://github.com/wsvincent/library.git
(.venv) > git push -u origin main
```

Heroku

The final step is to create a new project on Heroku and push our code into it. You should already be logged into Heroku via the command line from earlier in the chapter.

---

[50]https://github.com/new

You can either run `heroku create` and Heroku will randomly assign a name for your project or you can specify a custom name but it must be unique across all of Heroku! So the longer the better. I'm calling mine `wsvincent-library`. Prefixing your GitHub username is a good way to ensure you can specify the name of your Heroku project though you can always change it later on, too.

Shell

```
(.venv) > heroku create wsvincent-library
Creating ⬚ wsvincent-library... done
https://wsvincent-library.herokuapp.com/ | https://git.heroku.com/wsvincent-library.git
```

Then we'll push the code up to Heroku itself and add a web process so the dyno is running.

Shell

```
(.venv) > git push heroku main
(.venv) > heroku ps:scale web=1
```

The URL of your new app will be in the command line output or you can run `heroku open` to find it.

Here is my Library homepage.

Library Homepage

And also the API endpoint at `/api/`.

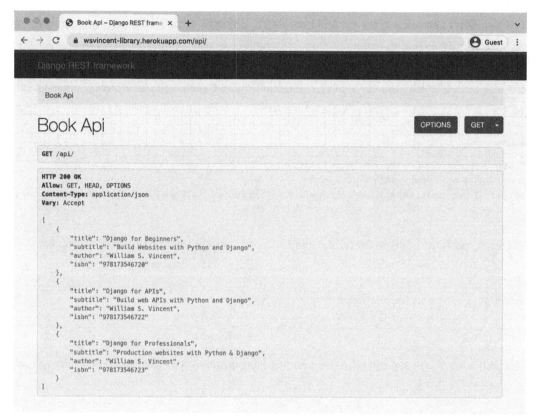

Library API

Deployment is a complicated topic and we've intentionally taken a number of shortcuts here. But the goal is to walkthrough a very basic Django website and API to show how it can be created from scratch.

Conclusion

We covered a lot of material in this chapter so don't worry if things feel a little confusing right now. We added Django REST Framework to our existing *Library* website and created an API endpoint for our books. Then we added tests and deployed our project to Heroku.

Web APIs can do a lot more than simply list information from your database though. In the next chapter we will build and deploy our own *Todo* API back-end that can be easily consumed by any front-end.

Chapter 5: Todo API

In this chapter we will build and deploy *Todo* API back-end that contains both a list API endpoint for all todos and dedicated endpoints for each individual todo. We will also learn about *Cross-Origin Resource Sharing* (CORS) which is a necessary security feature when a deployed back-end needs to communicate with a front-end. We have already made our first API and reviewed how HTTP and REST work in the abstract but it's still likely you don't "quite" see how it all fits together yet. By the end of these two chapters you will.

Single Page Apps (SPAs)

SPAs are required for mobile apps that run on iOS or Android and is the dominant pattern for web apps that want to take advantage of JavaScript front-end frameworks like React, Vue, Angular, and others.

There are multiple advantages to adopting a SPA approach. Developers can focus on their own area of expertise, typically either front-end or the back-end, but rarely both. It allows for using testing and build tools suitable to the task at hand since building, testing, and deploying a Django project is quite different than doing the same for a JavaScript one like React. And the forced separation removes the risk of coupling; it is not possible for front-end changes to break the back-end.

For large teams, SPAs make a lot of sense since there is already a built-in separation of tasks. Even in smaller teams, the adoption cost of an SPA approach is relatively small. The main risk of separating the back-end and the front-end is that it requires domain knowledge in both areas. While Django is relatively mature at this point the front-end ecosystem is decidedly not. A solo developer should think carefully about whether the added complexity of a dedicated JavaScript front-end is worth it versus sprinkling JavaScript into existing Django templates with modern tools like htmx[51].

---

[51]https://htmx.org/

Initial Set Up

The first step for any Django API is always to install Django and then later add Django REST
Framework on top of it. From the command line, navigate to the code directory on the Desktop
and create both a todo folder.

Shell

```
# Windows
> cd onedrive\desktop\code
> mkdir todo && cd todo

# macOS
% cd desktop/desktop/code
% mkdir todo && cd todo
```

Then run through the standard steps of creating a new virtual environment, activating it, and
installing Django.

Shell

```
# Windows
> python -m venv .venv
> .venv\Scripts\Activate.ps1
(.venv) > python -m pip install django~=4.0.0

# macOS
% python3 -m venv .venv
% source .venv/bin/activate
(.venv) % python3 -m pip install django~=4.0.0
```

Now that Django is installed we should start by creating a traditional Django project called
django_project, adding an app called todos within it, and then migrating the initial database.

Shell

Shell

```
(.venv) > django-admin startproject django_project .
(.venv) > python manage.py startapp todos
(.venv) > python manage.py migrate
```

In Django we always need to add new apps to our INSTALLED_APPS setting so do that now. Open up django_project/settings.py in your text editor and add todos to the bottom of the installed apps.

Code

```
# django_project/settings.py
INSTALLED_APPS = [
    "django.contrib.admin",
    "django.contrib.auth",
    "django.contrib.contenttypes",
    "django.contrib.sessions",
    "django.contrib.messages",
    "django.contrib.staticfiles",
    # Local
    "todos.apps.TodosConfig",  # new
]
```

If you run python manage.py runserver on the command line now and navigate in your web browser to http://127.0.0.1:8000/ you can see our project is successfully installed. We are ready to proceed.

.gitignore

Since we will be using Git for our source control it's important to create a .gitignore file early to specify what should *not be* tracked. This includes our new virtual environment .venv. To fix the issue, create a new file with your text editor called .gitignore and add a single line for .venv.

.gitignore

```
.venv/
```

Then let's initialize a new Git repository for our project and run `git status` to confirm the `.venv` file does not appear. We can also add all our setup work via `git add -A` and write our first commit message.

Shell

```
(.venv) > git status
(.venv) > git add -A
(.venv) > git commit -m "initial commit"
```

Models

Next up is defining the *Todo* database model within the `todos` app. We will keep things basic and have only two fields: `title` and `body`.

Code

```
# todos/models.py
from django.db import models


class Todo(models.Model):
    title = models.CharField(max_length=200)
    body = models.TextField()

    def __str__(self):
        return self.title
```

We import `models` at the top and then subclass it to create our own `Todo` model. A `__str__` method is also added to provide a human-readable name for each future model instance.

Since we have updated our model it's time for Django's two-step dance of making a new migration file and then syncing the database with the changes each time. On the command line type `Control+c` to stop our local server. Then run the `makemigrations` command.

Shell

```
(.venv) > python manage.py makemigrations todos
Migrations for 'todos':
  todos/migrations/0001_initial.py
    - Create model Todo
```

And then the `migrate` command.

Shell

```
(.venv) > python manage.py migrate
Operations to perform:
  Apply all migrations: admin, auth, contenttypes, sessions, todos
Running migrations:
  Applying todos.0001_initial... OK
```

It is optional to add the specific app we want to create a migration file for–we could instead type just `python manage.py makemigrations`–however it is a good best practice to adopt. Migration files are a fantastic way to debug applications and you should strive to create a migration file for each small change. If we had updated the models in two different apps and then run `python manage.py makemigrations` the resulting single migration file would contain data on *both* apps. That just makes debugging harder. Try to keep your migrations as small as possible.

Now we can use the built-in Django admin app to interact with our database. If we went into the admin straight away our `Todos` app would not appear. We need to explicitly add it via the `todos/admin.py` file. While we're at it we can create a `TodoAdmin` class that uses `list_display` so that both of our model fields, `title` and `body`, will be visible.

Code

```python
# todos/admin.py
from django.contrib import admin

from .models import Todo


class TodoAdmin(admin.ModelAdmin):
    list_display = (
        "title",
        "body",
    )


admin.site.register(Todo, TodoAdmin)
```

That's it! Now we can create a superuser account to log in to the admin.

Shell

```shell
(.venv) > python manage.py createsuperuser
```

Start up the local server again with `python manage.py runserver` and navigate to the admin section at `http://127.0.0.1:8000/admin/`. Log in and click on "+ Add" next to `Todos`. Create 3 new todo items, making sure to add a title and body for both. Here's what mine looks like:

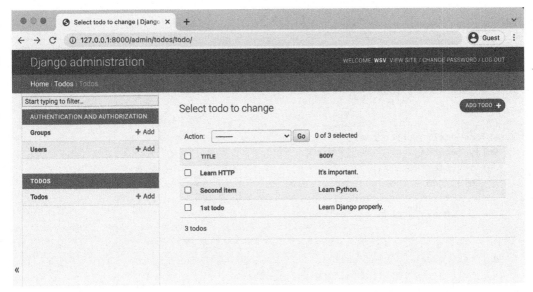

Admin todos

Tests

Code without tests is incomplete so we should add some now for our `Todo` model. We will use Django's TestCase[52] to create a test database and use `setUpTestData` to create test data for our `TodoModelTest` class. We want to confirm that the `title` and `body` appear as expected, as well as the `__str__` method on the model.

Open up the `todos/tests.py` file and fill it with the following:

---

[52]https://docs.djangoproject.com/en/4.0/topics/testing/tools/#testcase

Code

```
# todos/tests.py
from django.test import TestCase

from .models import Todo


class TodoModelTest(TestCase):
    @classmethod
    def setUpTestData(cls):
        cls.todo = Todo.objects.create(
            title="First Todo",
            body="A body of text here"
        )

    def test_model_content(self):
        self.assertEqual(self.todo.title, "First Todo")
        self.assertEqual(self.todo.body, "A body of text here")
        self.assertEqual(str(self.todo), "First Todo")
```

Make sure the local server is not running by typing `Control+c` from the command line and then run the test with the `python manage.py test` command.

Shell

```
(.venv) > python manage.py test
Creating test database for alias 'default'...
System check identified no issues (0 silenced).
..
----------------------------------------------------------------------
Ran 1 tests in 0.002s

OK
Destroying test database for alias 'default'...
```

We are actually done with the traditional Django part of our *Todo* API at this point! Since we are not bothering to build out webpages for this project all we need is a model and Django REST Framework will take care of the rest.

Django REST Framework

To add Django REST Framework stop the local server by typing `Control+c` and then install it with Pip.

Shell

```
(.venv) > python -m pip install djangorestframework~=3.13.0
```

Then add `rest_framework` to our `INSTALLED_APPS` setting just like any other third-party application. We also want to start configuring Django REST Framework specific settings which all exist under a configuration called `REST_FRAMEWORK` that can be added at the bottom of the file.

For starters, let's explicitly set permissions to AllowAny[53] which allows unrestricted access regardless of whether a request was authenticated or not. In a production setting API permissions are strictly controlled but for learning purposes we will use `AllowAny` for now.

Code

```python
# django_project/settings.py
INSTALLED_APPS = [
    "django.contrib.admin",
    "django.contrib.auth",
    "django.contrib.contenttypes",
    "django.contrib.sessions",
    "django.contrib.messages",
    "django.contrib.staticfiles",
    # 3rd party
    "rest_framework",  # new
    # Local
    "todos.apps.TodosConfig",
]

REST_FRAMEWORK = {
    "DEFAULT_PERMISSION_CLASSES": [
        "rest_framework.permissions.AllowAny",
    ],
}
```

---

[53]http://www.django-rest-framework.org/api-guide/permissions/#allowany

Django REST Framework has a lengthy list of implicitly set default settings. You can see the complete list here[54]. AllowAny is one of them which means that when we set it explicitly, as we did above, the effect is exactly the same as if we had no DEFAULT_PERMISSION_CLASSES config set.

Learning the default settings is something that takes time. We will become familiar with a number of them over the course of the book. The main takeaway to remember is that the implicit default settings are designed so that developers can jump in and start working quickly in a local development environment. Just as in traditional Django though, the default Django REST Framework settings are **not appropriate** for production. Before deployment we will typically make a number of changes to them over the course of a project.

Ok, so Django REST Framework is installed. What next? Unlike the *Library* project in the previous chapters where we built both a webpage **and** an API, here we are just building an API. Therefore we do not need to create any template files or traditional Django views. It is also arguably unnecessary to create a separate apis app since this project is API-first by design. While Django comes with a lot of guardrails around project structure, it is up to the developer to decide how to organize their apps. This is a common point of confusion for newcomers but by building multiple projects with different app structures it becomes clearer that apps are just an organizational tool for the developer. As long as an app is added to INSTALLED_APPS and uses the correct import structure they can be used in almost any configuration.

To transform our existing database model into a web API we will need to update the URLs, add Django Rest Framework views, and create a serializer. Let's begin!

URLs

I like to start with the URLs first since they are the entry-point for our API endpoints. Start at the Django project-level file located at django_project/urls.py. We will import include on the second line and add a route for our todos app at the path of api/. It is a good idea to have all API endpoints at a consistent path such as api/ in case you decide to add traditional Django webpages at a later date.

---

[54]http://www.django-rest-framework.org/api-guide/settings/

Code

```
# django_project/urls.py
from django.contrib import admin
from django.urls import path, include    # new


urlpatterns = [
    path("admin/", admin.site.urls),
    path("api/", include("todos.urls")),  # new
]
```

Next create an app-level todos/urls.py file with your text editor and add the following code:

Code

```
# todos/urls.py
from django.urls import path

from .views import ListTodo, DetailTodo

urlpatterns = [
    path("<int:pk>/", DetailTodo.as_view(), name="todo_detail"),
    path("", ListTodo.as_view(), name="todo_list"),
]
```

Note that we are referencing two views here, ListTodo and DetailTodo, that we have yet to create. But the routing is now complete. There will be a list of all todos at the empty string "", in other words at api/, and each individual todo will be available at its primary key, pk, which is a value Django sets automatically in every database table. The first entry is 1, the second is 2, and so on. Therefore our first todo will eventually be located at the API endpoint api/1/, the second at api/2/, and so on.

Serializers

Let's review where we are so far. We started with a traditional Django project, added a dedicated app, configured our database model, and added initial data. Then we installed Django REST Framework and created an api app for which we just configured our URLs. There are two steps remaining: serializer and views. Let's begin with the serializer which transforms our model data into JSON that will be outputted at our desired URLs. Create a new file called `todos/serializers.py` file and update it with the following code.

Code

```
# todos/serializers.py
from rest_framework import serializers

from .models import Todo


class TodoSerializer(serializers.ModelSerializer):
    class Meta:
        model = Todo
        fields = (
            "id",
            "title",
            "body",
        )
```

At the top we have imported `serializers` from Django REST Framework along with our `Todo` database model. Then we extended `ModelSerializer` into a new class called `TodoSerializer`. The format here is very similar to how we create model classes or forms in Django itself. We're specifying which model to use and the specific fields on it we want to expose. Remember that `id` (similar to a `pk`) is created automatically by Django so we didn't have to define it in our Todo model but we will display in our individual detail view for each todo. And that's it! Django REST Framework will magically transform our data into JSON exposing the fields for `id`, `title`, and `body` from our `Todo` model.

What's the difference between `id` and `pk`? They both refer to a field automatically added to Django models by the ORM. id[55] is a built-in function from the Python standard library while pk[56] comes from Django itself. Generic class-based views like DetailView in Django expect to be passed a parameter named `pk` while on model fields it is often common to simply refer to `id`.

The last thing we need to do is configure a `views.py` file to accompany our serializer and URLs.

---

[55]https://docs.python.org/3.10/library/functions.html#id
[56]https://docs.djangoproject.com/en/4.0/ref/models/instances/#the-pk-property

Views

We will use two DRF generic views here: ListAPIView[57] to display all todos and RetrieveAPIView[58] to display a single model instance.

Update the todos/views.py file to look as follows:

Code

```python
# todos/views.py
from rest_framework import generics

from .models import Todo
from .serializers import TodoSerializer


class ListTodo(generics.ListAPIView):
    queryset = Todo.objects.all()
    serializer_class = TodoSerializer


class DetailTodo(generics.RetrieveAPIView):
    queryset = Todo.objects.all()
    serializer_class = TodoSerializer
```

At the top we import Django REST Framework's generics views, our Todo model and the TodoSerializer we just created. Recall from our todos/urls.py file that we have two routes and therefore two distinct views. A new view called ListTodo subclasses ListAPIView while DetailTodo subclasses RetrieveAPIView.

Astute readers will notice that there is a bit of redundancy in the code here. We essentially repeat the queryset and serializer_class for each view, even though the generic view extended is different. Later on in the book we will learn about viewsets and routers which address this issue and allow us to create the same API views and URLs with much less code.

But for now we're done! Our API is ready to consume.

---

[57]http://www.django-rest-framework.org/api-guide/generic-views/#listapiview

[58]http://www.django-rest-framework.org/api-guide/generic-views/#retrieveapiview

Browsable API

Let's use Django REST Framework's browsable API now to interact with our data. Make sure the local server is running and navigate to `http://127.0.0.1:8000/api/` to see our working API list views endpoint.

API List

This page shows the three todos we created earlier in the database model. An API *endpoint* refers to the URL used to make a request. If there are multiple items at an endpoint it is known as a *collection* while a single item is known as a *resource*. The terms endpoint and resource are often used interchangeably by developers but they mean different things.

We also made a `DetailTodo` view for each individual model which should be visible at:

`http://127.0.0.1:8000/api/1/.`

Shell

```
(.venv) > python manage.py test
Creating test database for alias 'default'...
System check identified no issues (0 silenced).
..
----------------------------------------------------------------
Ran 3 tests in 0.007s

OK
Destroying test database for alias 'default'...
```

We're almost done now but there are two additional considerations since our backend will be communicating with a frontend on a different port. This raises a host of security concerns that we will now tackle.

CORS

Cross-Origin Resource Sharing (CORS)[59] refers to the fact that whenever a client interacts with an API hosted on a different domain (mysite.com vs yoursite.com) or port (localhost:3000 vs localhost:8000) there are potential security issues.

Specifically, CORS requires the web server to include specific HTTP headers that allow for the client to determine if and when cross-domain requests should be allowed. Because we are using a SPA architecture the front-end will be on a different local port during development and a completely different domain once deployed!

The easiest way to handle this issue--and the one recommended by Django REST Framework[60]--is to use middleware that will automatically include the appropriate HTTP headers based on our settings. The third-party package django-cors-headers[61] is the default choice within the Django community and can easily added to our existing project.

Make sure to stop the local server with Control+c and then install django-cors-headers with Pip.

---

[59]https://developer.mozilla.org/en-US/docs/Web/HTTP/CORS
[60]http://www.django-rest-framework.org/topics/ajax-csrf-cors/
[61]https://github.com/adamchainz/django-cors-headers

Shell

```
(.venv) > python -m pip install django-cors-headers~=3.10.0
```

Next update our django_project/settings.py file in three places:

- add corsheaders to the INSTALLED_APPS
- add CorsMiddleware above CommonMiddleWare in MIDDLEWARE
- create a CORS_ALLOWED_ORIGINS config at the bottom of the file

Code

```python
# django_project/settings.py
INSTALLED_APPS = [
    "django.contrib.admin",
    "django.contrib.auth",
    "django.contrib.contenttypes",
    "django.contrib.sessions",
    "django.contrib.messages",
    "django.contrib.staticfiles",
    # 3rd party
    "rest_framework",
    "corsheaders",  # new
    # Local
    "todos.apps.TodosConfig",
]

MIDDLEWARE = [
    "django.middleware.security.SecurityMiddleware",
    "django.contrib.sessions.middleware.SessionMiddleware",
    "corsheaders.middleware.CorsMiddleware",  # new
    "django.middleware.common.CommonMiddleware",
    "django.middleware.csrf.CsrfViewMiddleware",
    "django.contrib.auth.middleware.AuthenticationMiddleware",
    "django.contrib.messages.middleware.MessageMiddleware",
    "django.middleware.clickjacking.XFrameOptionsMiddleware",
]

CORS_ALLOWED_ORIGINS = (
    "http://localhost:3000",
    "http://localhost:8000",
)
```

It's very important that `corsheaders.middleware.CorsMiddleware` appears in the proper location since Django middlewares are loaded top-to-bottom. Also note that we've whitelisted two domains: `localhost:3000` and `localhost:8000`. The former is the default port for React (if that is the front-end being used) and the latter is the default Django port.

CSRF

Just as CORS is an issue when dealing with a SPA architecture, so too are forms. Django comes with robust CSRF protection[62] that should be added to forms in any Django template, but with a dedicated React front-end setup this protection isn't inherently available. Fortunately, we can allow specific cross-domain requests from our frontend by setting CSRF_TRUSTED_ORIGINS[63].

At the bottom of the `settings.py` file, next to `CORS_ORIGIN_WHITELIST`, add this additional line for React's default local port of 3000:

Code

```
# django_project/settings.py
CSRF_TRUSTED_ORIGINS = ["localhost:3000"]
```

And that's it! Our back-end is now complete and capable of communicating with any front-end that uses port 3000. If our front-end of choice dictates a different port that can easily be updated in our code.

Back-End API Deployment

We will again deploy the Django API backend with Heroku. If you recall our deployment checklist from Chapter 4 for the Library API included the following:

- configure static files and install `WhiteNoise`
- install `Gunicorn` as the production web server
- create `requirements.txt`, `runtime.txt`, and `Procfile` files

---

[62]https://docs.djangoproject.com/en/4.0/ref/csrf/
[63]https://docs.djangoproject.com/en/4.0/ref/settings/#csrf-trusted-origins

- update the ALLOWED_HOSTS configuration

We can run through each of these more quickly now. For static files create a new static directory from the terminal shell.

Shell

```
(.venv) > mkdir static
```

With your text editor create a .keep file within the static directory so it is picked up by Git. Then install whitenoise to handle static files in production.

Shell

```
(.venv) > python -m pip install whitenoise==5.3.0
```

WhiteNoise must be added to django_project/settings.py in the following locations:

- whitenoise above django.contrib.staticfiles in INSTALLED_APPS
- WhiteNoiseMiddleware above CommonMiddleware
- STATICFILES_STORAGE configuration pointing to WhiteNoise

Code

```
# django_project/settings.py
INSTALLED_APPS = [
    ...
    "whitenoise.runserver_nostatic",  # new
    "django.contrib.staticfiles",
]

MIDDLEWARE = [
    "django.middleware.security.SecurityMiddleware",
    "django.contrib.sessions.middleware.SessionMiddleware",
    "whitenoise.middleware.WhiteNoiseMiddleware",  # new
    "corsheaders.middleware.CorsMiddleware",
    ...
]

STATIC_URL = "/static/"
```

```
STATICFILES_DIRS = [str(BASE_DIR.joinpath("static"))]  # new
STATIC_ROOT = str(BASE_DIR.joinpath("staticfiles"))  # new
STATICFILES_STORAGE =
    "whitenoise.storage.CompressedManifestStaticFilesStorage"  # new
```

Finally run the collectstatic command so that all static directories and files are compiled into one location for deployment purposes.

Shell

```
(.venv) > python manage.py collectstatic
```

Gunicorn will be used as the production web server and can be installed directly.

Shell

```
(.venv) > python -m pip install gunicorn~=20.1.0
```

With your text editor create a runtime.txt file in the project root directory next to manage.py. It will have one line specifying the version of Python to run on Heroku.

runtime.txt

```
python-3.10.2
```

Now create an empty Procfile file in the same project root directory location. It should contain the following single line command:

Procfile

```
web: gunicorn django_project.wsgi --log-file -
```

We can automatically generate a requirements.txt file with the contents of our virtual environment in one command:

Shell

```
(.venv) > python -m pip freeze > requirements.txt
```

The last step is to update the `ALLOWED_HOSTS` configuration in `django_project/settings.py`. Access should be restricted to `localhost`, `127.0.0.1`, and `.herokuapp.com`.

Code

```
# django_project/settings.py
ALLOWED_HOSTS = [".herokuapp.com", "localhost", "127.0.0.1"]
```

Make sure to add and commit the new changes to Git.

Shell

```
(.venv) > git status
(.venv) > git add -A
(.venv) > git commit -m "New updates for Heroku deployment"
```

Then log into Heroku's CLI by typing the command `heroku login` which will require you to verify credentials on the Heroku website itself.

Shell

```
(.venv) > heroku login
heroku: Press any key to open up the browser to login or q to exit:
Opening browser to ...
Logging in... done
Logged in as will@wsvincent.com
```

Once logged in we need to create a new Heroku project. Since Heroku names are unique you will need to come up with your own variation. I've called mine `wsvincent-todo`.

Shell

```
(.venv) > heroku create wsvincent-todo
Creating ⬚ wsvincent-todo... done
https://wsvincent-todo.herokuapp.com/ | https://git.heroku.com/wsvincent-todo.git
```

Push the code up to Heroku and add a web process so the dyno is running.

Shell

```
(.venv) > git push heroku main
(.venv) > heroku ps:scale web=1
```

The URL of your new app will be in the command line output or you can run `heroku open` to find it. Make sure to navigate to the `/api/` endpoint to see a list of all Todo items. Here is my Todo API endpoint listing all items:

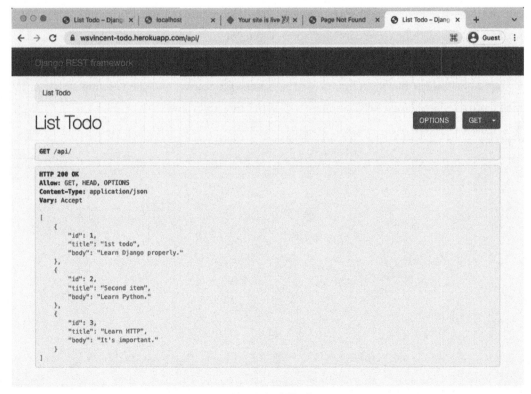

Todo API List Endpoint

The individual API endpoints for each Todo item will also be available at `/api/1/`, `/api/2/`, and so on. The deployed Todo API is now consumable. Once the deployed URLs of the front-end code is known they can be added to the `CORS` and `CSRF` sections as appropriate.

Conclusion

With a minimal amount of code Django REST Framework has allowed us to create a Django API from scratch. Unlike our example in the previous chapter, we did not build out any web pages for this project since our goal was just to create an API. However at any point in the future, we easily could! It would just require adding a new view, URL, and a template to expose our existing database model.

An important point in this example is that we added CORS headers and explicitly set only the domains `localhost:3000` and `localhost:8000` to have access to our API. Correctly setting CORS headers is an easy thing to be confused about when you first start building APIs.

There's much more configuration we can and will do later on but at the end of the day creating Django APIs is about making a model, writing some URL routes, and then adding a little bit of magic provided by Django REST Framework's serializers and views.

Chapter 6: Blog API

The major project in this book is a *Blog* API using the full set of Django REST Framework features. It will have users, permissions, and allow for full CRUD (Create-Read-Update-Delete) functionality. We'll also explore viewsets, routers, and documentation.

In this chapter we will build the basic API section. Just as with our *Library* and *Todo* APIs, we start with traditional Django and then add in Django REST Framework. The main differences are we'll be using a custom user model and supporting CRUD operations from the beginning which, as we will see, Django REST Framework makes quite seamless to do.

Initial Set Up

Our set up is the same as before. Navigate into the `code` directory and within it create one for this project called `blogapi`. Then install Django in a new virtual environment and create a new Django project called `django_project`.

Shell

```
# Windows
> cd onedrive\desktop\code
> mkdir blogapi
> cd blogapi
> python -m venv .venv
> .venv\Scripts\Activate.ps1
(.venv) > python -m pip install django~=4.0.0
(.venv) > django-admin startproject django_project .

# macOS
% cd desktop/desktop/code
% mkdir blogapi
% cd blogapi
% python3 -m venv .venv
% source .venv/bin/activate
(.venv) % python3 -m pip install django~=4.0.0
(.venv) % django-admin startproject django_project .
```

Run the command `python manage.py runserver` and it should bring up the Django welcome page over at `http://127.0.0.1:8000/`.

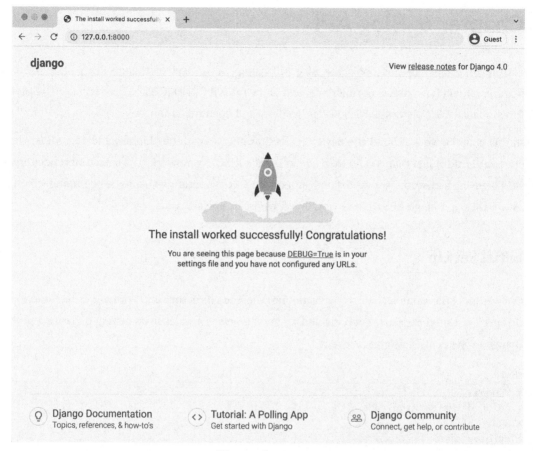

Django welcome page

The terminal shell likely displays a message complaining `You have 18 unapplied migration(s)`. We are deliberately *not* running `migrate` yet because we'll be using a custom user model and want to wait until it is configured before running our first `migrate` command.

.gitignore

Using Git early and often is always a good idea on projects. It lets developers track the progress of the project over time and identify any errors that may arise. Let's initialize a new Git repo and check its status.

Shell

```
(.venv) > git init
(.venv) > git status
```

The `.venv` file should appear which we do not want in source control therefore use your text editor to create a `.gitignore` file in the project directory next to the `manage.py` file. Add a single line for `.venv` so it will be ignored by Git.

.gitignore

```
.venv/
```

Then run `git status` again to confirm `.venv` no longer appears, add our current work, and create the first Git commit.

Shell

```
(.venv) > git status
(.venv) > git add -A
(.venv) > git commit -m "initial commit"
```

Custom User Model

Adding a custom user model is an optional but recommended next step. Even if you have no plans to use one, taking a few steps now leaves the door open to leveraging it in the future on your project.

To do so first create a new app called `accounts`.

Shell

```
(.venv) > python manage.py startapp accounts
```

Then add it to our INSTALLED_APPS configuration so Django knows it exists.

Code

```
# django_project/settings.py
INSTALLED_APPS = [
    "django.contrib.admin",
    "django.contrib.auth",
    "django.contrib.contenttypes",
    "django.contrib.sessions",
    "django.contrib.messages",
    "django.contrib.staticfiles",
    # Local
    "accounts.apps.AccountsConfig",  # new
]
```

Within accounts/models.py define a custom user model called CustomUser by extending AbstractUser[64] and adding a single field, name, for now. We'll also add a __str__ method to return the user's email address in the admin and elsewhere.

Code

```
# accounts/models.py
from django.contrib.auth.models import AbstractUser
from django.db import models


class CustomUser(AbstractUser):
    name = models.CharField(null=True, blank=True, max_length=100)
```

The last step is to update the AUTH_USER_MODEL[65] configuration in settings.py, which is implicitly set to auth.User, over to accounts.CustomUser. This can be added at the bottom of the file.

---

[64]https://docs.djangoproject.com/en/4.0/topics/auth/customizing/#django.contrib.auth.models.AbstractUser
[65]https://docs.djangoproject.com/en/4.0/ref/settings/#auth-user-model

Code

```
# django_project/settings.py
AUTH_USER_MODEL   = "accounts.CustomUser"   # new
```

Now we can run `makemigrations` for our model changes, `migrate` to initialize the database, and `createsuperuser` to create a superuser account so we can view the admin. Make sure to include an `email` for your custom user.

Shell

```
(.venv) > python manage.py makemigrations
(.venv) > python manage.py migrate
(.venv) > python manage.py createsuperuser
```

Then launch Django's internal web server with the `runserver` command:

Shell

```
(.venv) > python manage.py runserver
```

If we head on over to the admin at `http://127.0.0.1:8000/admin/` and log in it looks like something is missing doesn't it?

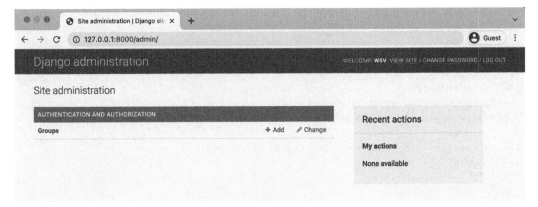

Admin Empty Homepage

Only the `Groups` section appears. We don't have `Users` as we normally would with the default User model. What's missing is two things: we have to customize `accounts/admin.py` to display our new custom user model and create a new file called `accounts/forms.py` that sets `CustomUser` to be used when creating or changing users. We'll start with `account/forms.py`.

Code

```
# accounts/forms.py
from django.contrib.auth.forms import UserCreationForm, UserChangeForm

from .models import CustomUser


class CustomUserCreationForm(UserCreationForm):
    class Meta(UserCreationForm):
        model = CustomUser
        fields = UserCreationForm.Meta.fields + ("name",)


class CustomUserChangeForm(UserChangeForm):
    class Meta:
        model = CustomUser
        fields = UserChangeForm.Meta.fields
```

At the top we import UserCreationForm[66] and UserChangeForm[67] which are used for creating or updating a user. We'll also import our CustomUser model so that it can be integrated into new CustomUserCreationForm and CustomUserChangeForm classes.

With that out of the way, the last step in the custom user setup is to update accounts/admin.py to properly display the new custom user.

Code

```
# accounts/admin.py
from django.contrib import admin
from django.contrib.auth.admin import UserAdmin

from .forms import CustomUserCreationForm, CustomUserChangeForm
from .models import CustomUser


class CustomUserAdmin(UserAdmin):
    add_form = CustomUserCreationForm
    form = CustomUserChangeForm
    model = CustomUser
    list_display = [
```

[66]https://docs.djangoproject.com/en/4.0/topics/auth/default/#django.contrib.auth.forms.UserCreationForm
[67]https://docs.djangoproject.com/en/4.0/topics/auth/default/#django.contrib.auth.forms.UserChangeForm

```
        "email",
        "username",
        "name",
        "is_staff",
    ]
    fieldsets = UserAdmin.fieldsets + ((None, {"fields": ("name",)}),)
    add_fieldsets = UserAdmin.add_fieldsets + ((None, {"fields": ("name",)}),)


admin.site.register(CustomUser, CustomUserAdmin)
```

And we're done. If you reload the admin page it now displays Users.

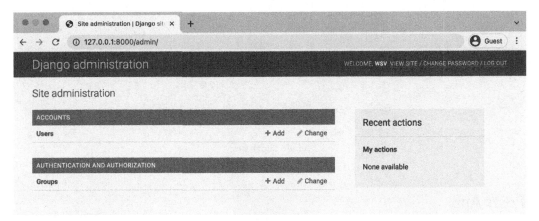

Admin Users

If you click on Users you can see our superuser is in there, too.

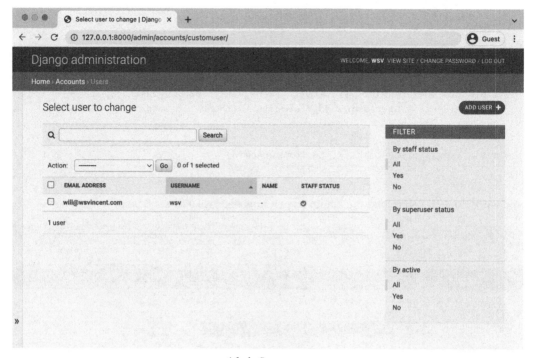

Admin Superuser

Posts App

It's time to create a dedicated app for our Blog. Naming is always tricky and while it is tempting to add a new app called `blog` and a related model called `Blog`, this is rarely done since multiple areas within Django add an `s` on to app and model names and "blogs" just doesn't look very good. For this reason, it is more common to called a Blog app something like `posts` and the related database model simply `Post`. That's what we'll do here.

Type `Control+c` to stop the local server and then use the management command `startapp` to create the new `posts` app.

Shell

```
(.venv) > python manage.py startapp posts
```

Then immediately update INSTALLED_APPS in the django_project/settings.py file before we forget.

Code

```
# django_project/settings.py
INSTALLED_APPS = [
    "django.contrib.admin",
    "django.contrib.auth",
    "django.contrib.contenttypes",
    "django.contrib.sessions",
    "django.contrib.messages",
    "django.contrib.staticfiles",
    # Local
    "accounts.apps.AccountsConfig",
    "posts.apps.PostsConfig",  # new
]
```

Post Model

Our blog Post database model will have five fields: author, title, body, created_at, and updated_at. We will also import Django's settings so we can refer to AUTH_USER_MODEL in our author field. And we'll add a __str__ method as a general best practice.

Code

```
# posts/models.py
from django.conf import settings
from django.db import models


class Post(models.Model):
    title = models.CharField(max_length=50)
    body = models.TextField()
    author = models.ForeignKey(settings.AUTH_USER_MODEL, on_delete=models.CASCADE)
    created_at = models.DateTimeField(auto_now_add=True)
    updated_at = models.DateTimeField(auto_now=True)

    def __str__(self):
        return self.title
```

That looks straightforward enough. Now update our database by first creating a new migration file with the command `makemigrations posts` and then running `migrate` to sync the database with our model changes.

Shell

```
(.venv) > python manage.py makemigrations posts
(.venv) > python manage.py migrate
```

Good! We want to view our data in Django's admin app so we'll quickly update `posts/admin.py` as follows.

Code

```
# posts/admin.py
from django.contrib import admin

from .models import Post

admin.site.register(Post)
```

Start up the local web server again with `python manage.py runserver` and visit the admin to see our work in action.

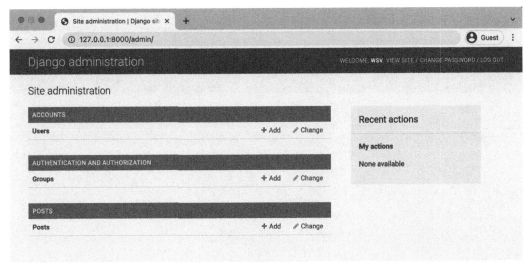

Admin Posts

There's our Posts app! Click on the "+ Add" button next to Posts and create a new blog post. Next to "Author" will be a dropdown menu that has your superuser account (mine is called wsv). Make sure an author is selected, add a title, add body content, and then click on the "Save" button.

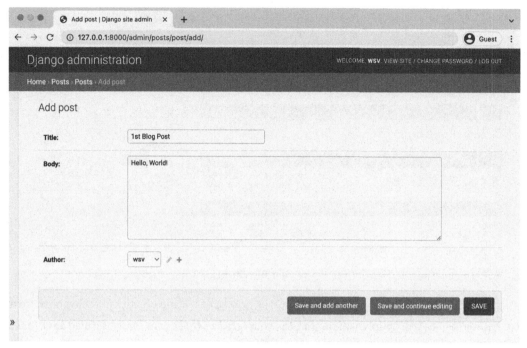

Admin add blog post

You will be redirected to the Posts page which displays all existing blog posts.

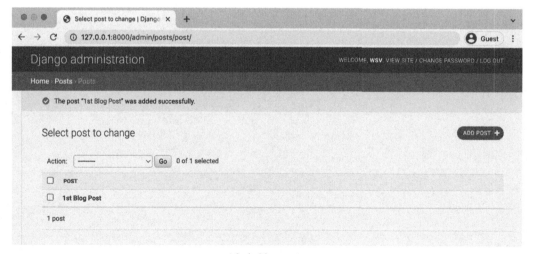

Admin blog posts

Tests

We've written new code so it is time for tests. These are added to the existing `posts/tests.py` file created with the `startapp` command.

At the top of the file import get_user_model()[68] to refer to our User along with `TestCase` and the `Post` model. Then create a class `BlogTests` with set up data and a single test for now, `test_-post_model`, that checks the fields on the `Post` model along with its `__str__` method.

Code

```
# posts/tests.py
from django.contrib.auth import get_user_model
from django.test import TestCase

from .models import Post


class BlogTests(TestCase):
    @classmethod
    def setUpTestData(cls):
        cls.user = get_user_model().objects.create_user(
            username="testuser",
            email="test@email.com",
            password="secret",
        )

        cls.post = Post.objects.create(
            author=cls.user,
            title="A good title",
            body="Nice body content",
        )

    def test_post_model(self):
        self.assertEqual(self.post.author.username, "testuser")
        self.assertEqual(self.post.title, "A good title")
        self.assertEqual(self.post.body, "Nice body content")
        self.assertEqual(str(self.post), "A good title")
```

To confirm that our tests are working quit the local server with `Control+c` and run our tests.

[68]https://docs.djangoproject.com/en/4.0/topics/auth/customizing/#django.contrib.auth.get_user_model

Shell

```
(.venv) > python manage.py test
Creating test database for alias 'default'...
System check identified no issues (0 silenced).
.
----------------------------------------------------------------------
Ran 1 test in 0.105s

OK
Destroying test database for alias 'default'...
```

We are done now with the regular Django part of our API. All we really need is a model and some data in our database. Now it's time to add Django REST Framework to take care of transforming our model data into an API.

Django REST Framework

As we have seen before, Django REST Framework takes care of the heavy lifting of transforming our database models into a RESTful API. There are three main steps to this process:

- `urls.py` file for the URL routes
- `serializers.py` file to transform the data into JSON
- `views.py` file to apply logic to each API endpoint

On the command line use `pip` to install Django REST Framework.

Shell

```
(.venv) > python -m pip install djangorestframework~=3.13.0
```

Then add it to the `INSTALLED_APPS` section of our `django_project/settings.py` file. It's also a good idea to explicitly set our permissions. By default Django REST Framework is configured to `AllowAny` to enable ease of us in local development however this is far from secure. We will update this permission setting in the next chapter.

Code

```
# django_project/settings.py
INSTALLED_APPS = [
    "django.contrib.admin",
    "django.contrib.auth",
    "django.contrib.contenttypes",
    "django.contrib.sessions",
    "django.contrib.messages",
    "django.contrib.staticfiles",
    # 3rd-party apps
    "rest_framework",  # new
    # Local
    "accounts.apps.AccountsConfig",
    "posts.apps.PostsConfig",
]

REST_FRAMEWORK = {  # new
    "DEFAULT_PERMISSION_CLASSES": [
        "rest_framework.permissions.AllowAny",
    ],
}
```

Now we need to create our URLs, views, and serializers.

URLs

Let's start with the URL routes for the actual location of the endpoints. Update the project-level urls.py file with the include import on the second line and a new api/v1/ route for our posts app.

Code

```
# django_project/urls.py
from django.contrib import admin
from django.urls import path, include  # new


urlpatterns = [
    path("admin/", admin.site.urls),
    path("api/v1/", include("posts.urls")),  # new
]
```

It is a good practice to always version your APIs since when you make a large change there may be some lag time before various consumers of the API can also update. That way you can support a v1 of an API for a period of time while also launching a new, updated v2 and avoid breaking other apps that rely on your API back-end.

Note that since our only app at this point is posts we can include it directly here. If we had multiple apps in a project it might make more sense to create a dedicated api app and then include all the other API url routes into it. But for basic projects like this one, I prefer to avoid an api app that is just used for routing. We can always add one later, if needed.

Next create a new posts/urls.py file and add the following code:

Code

```
# posts/urls.py
from django.urls import path

from .views import PostList, PostDetail

urlpatterns = [
    path("<int:pk>/", PostDetail.as_view(), name="post_detail"),
    path("", PostList.as_view(), name="post_list"),
]
```

At the top of the file we imported two views—PostList and PostDetail—that we will write in the next section but they correspond to a list of all blog posts at the empty string, "", which means at api/v1/. The individual detail posts will be at their primary key, pk, so the first blog post will be at api/v1/1/, the second at api/v1/2/, and so on. So far this is all standard Django stuff.

Serializers

Now for our serializers. Create a new posts/serializers.py file with your text editor. The serializer not only transforms data into JSON, it can also specify which fields to include or exclude. In our case, we will include the id field Django automatically adds to database models but we will *exclude* the updated_at field by not including it in our fields.

The ability to include/exclude fields in our API this easily is a remarkable feature. More often than not, an underlying database model will have far more fields than what needs to be exposed. Django REST Framework's powerful serializer class makes it extremely straightforward to control this.

Code

```python
# posts/serializers.py
from rest_framework import serializers

from .models import Post


class PostSerializer(serializers.ModelSerializer):
    class Meta:
        fields = (
            "id",
            "author",
            "title",
            "body",
            "created_at",
        )
        model = Post
```

At the top of the file we have imported Django REST Framework's serializers class and our own models. Then we created a PostSerializer and added a Meta class where we specified which fields to include and explicitly set the model, Post, to use. There are many ways to customize a serializer but for common use cases, such as a basic blog, this is all we need.

Views

The final step is to create our views. Django REST Framework has several generic views that are helpful. We have already used ListAPIView[69] in both the *Library* and *Todos* APIs to create a **read-only** endpoint collection, essentially a list of all model instances. In the *Todos* API we used RetrieveAPIView[70] for a read-only single endpoint, which is analogous to a detail view in traditional Django.

For our *Blog* API we want to list all available blog posts as a read-write endpoint which means using ListCreateAPIView[71], which is similar to the ListAPIView we've used previously but allows for writes and therefore POST requests. We also want to make the individual blog posts available to be read, updated, or deleted. And sure enough, there is a built-in generic Django REST Framework view just for this purpose: RetrieveUpdateDestroyAPIView[72]. That's what we'll use here.

Update the posts/views.py file as follows.

Code

```
# posts/views.py
from rest_framework import generics

from .models import Post
from .serializers import PostSerializer


class PostList(generics.ListCreateAPIView):
    queryset = Post.objects.all()
    serializer_class = PostSerializer


class PostDetail(generics.RetrieveUpdateDestroyAPIView):
    queryset = Post.objects.all()
    serializer_class = PostSerializer
```

---

[69]http://www.django-rest-framework.org/api-guide/generic-views/#listapiview
[70]http://www.django-rest-framework.org/api-guide/generic-views/#retrieveapiview
[71]http://www.django-rest-framework.org/api-guide/generic-views/#listcreateapiview
[72]http://www.django-rest-framework.org/api-guide/generic-views/#retrieveupdatedestroyapiview

At the top of the file we import `generics` from Django REST Framework as well as our models and serializers files. Then we create two views: `PostList` uses the generic `ListCreateAPIView` while `PostDetail` uses the `RetrieveUpdateDestroyAPIView`.

It's pretty amazing that all we have to do is update our generic view to radically change the behavior of a given API endpoint. This is the advantage of using a full-featured framework like Django REST Framework: all of this functionality is available, tested, and *just works*. As developers we do not have to reinvent the wheel here.

Phew. Our API is now complete and we really did not have to write much code on our own. We will make additional improvements to our API in the coming chapters but it is worth appreciating that it already performs the basic list and CRUD functionality we desire. Time to test things out with the Django Rest Framework's browsable API.

Browsable API

Start up the local server to interact with our API.

Shell

```
(.venv) > python manage.py runserver
```

Then go to `http://127.0.0.1:8000/api/v1/` to see the Post List endpoint.

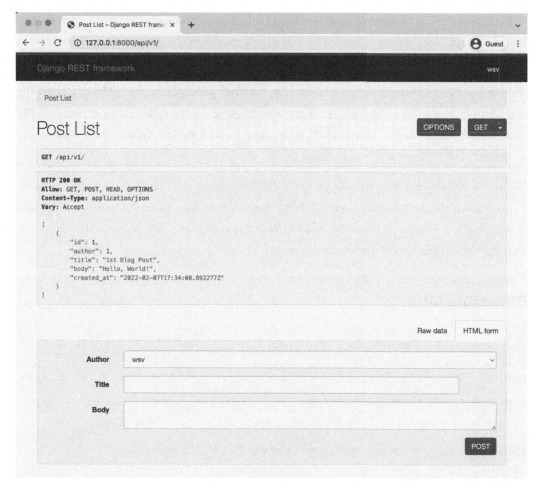

API Post List

The page displays a list of our blog posts—just one at the moment—in JSON format. Note that both GET and POST methods are allowed. The id is 1 representing this is the 1st blog post and the author is also 1 since we used a superuser account which was the first created. It might be more ideal to display the username or perhaps require a full name to be displayed.

Serializers are very powerful and can be customized to output almost whatever we want with whatever restrictions in place. There are many listed in the docs[73] which also note that "REST Framework does not attempt to automatically optimize querysets passed to serializers in terms

---

[73]https://www.django-rest-framework.org/api-guide/relations/#serializer-relations

of select_related and prefetch_related since it would be too much magic." On larger sites serializers usually need to be tweaked for performance reasons.

Unlike our previous APIs for the blog we have a model instance endpoint displaying a single post. Let's confirm that it also exists by navigating to http://127.0.0.1:8000/api/v1/1/ in the web browser.

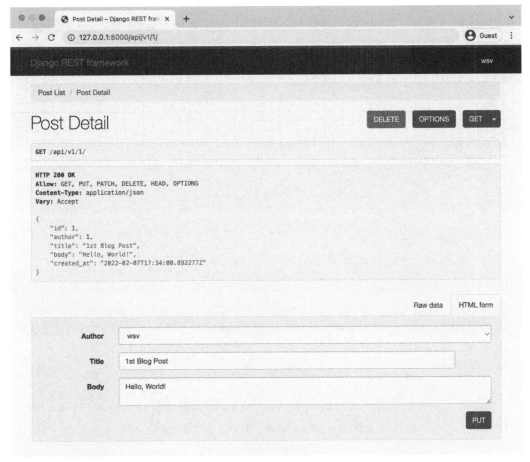

API Post Detail

You can see in the header that GET, PUT, PATCH, and DELETE are supported but not POST. And in fact you can use the HTML form below to make changes or even use the red "DELETE" button to delete the instance.

Let's try things out. Update our title with the additional text (edited) at the end. Then click on the "PUT" button.

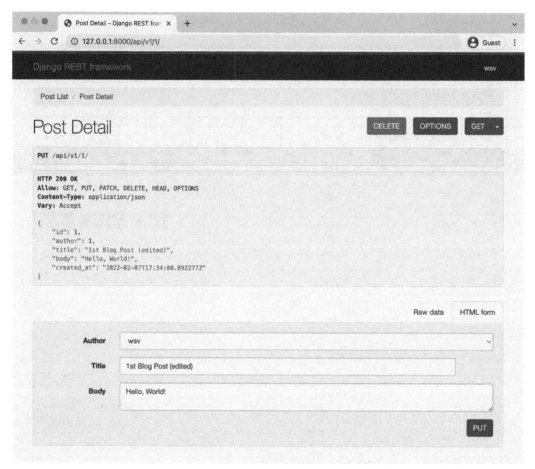

API Post Detail edited

Go back to the Post List view by clicking on the link for it at the top of the page or navigating directly to `http://127.0.0.1:8000/api/v1/` and you can see the updated text there as well.

API Post List edited

CORS

Since it is likely our API will be consumed on another domain we should configure CORS and set which domains will have access. As we saw in the earlier Todo API the process is straightforward. First, we'll stop the local web server with Control+c and install the third-party package django-cors-headers[74].

---

[74]https://github.com/adamchainz/django-cors-headers

Shell

```
(.venv) > python -m pip install django-cors-headers~=3.10.0
```

Then we add `corsheaders` to `INSTALLED_APPS`, add `CorsMiddleware` to the `MIDDLEWARE` setting, and create a `CORS_ALLOWED_ORIGINS` list. Update the `settings.py` file as follows to do all three:

Code

```python
# django_project/settings.py
INSTALLED_APPS = [
    "django.contrib.admin",
    "django.contrib.auth",
    "django.contrib.contenttypes",
    "django.contrib.sessions",
    "django.contrib.messages",
    "django.contrib.staticfiles",
    # 3rd party
    "rest_framework",
    "corsheaders",  # new
    # Local
    "accounts.apps.AccountsConfig",
    "posts.apps.PostsConfig",
]


MIDDLEWARE = [
    "django.middleware.security.SecurityMiddleware",
    "django.contrib.sessions.middleware.SessionMiddleware",
    "corsheaders.middleware.CorsMiddleware",  # new
    "django.middleware.common.CommonMiddleware",
    "django.middleware.csrf.CsrfViewMiddleware",
    "django.contrib.auth.middleware.AuthenticationMiddleware",
    "django.contrib.messages.middleware.MessageMiddleware",
    "django.middleware.clickjacking.XFrameOptionsMiddleware",
]

# new
CORS_ORIGIN_WHITELIST = (
    "http://localhost:3000",
    "http://localhost:8000",
)
```

In the event our API is used with forms it is a good idea to allow specific cross-domain requests from our frontend by setting CSRF_TRUSTED_ORIGINS[75] as well. We can do this in `settings.py` right after the `CORS_ORIGIN_WHITELIST` section. For now we'll set it to local port of 3000, which is what React uses, though we can easily change the port in the future depending on our front-end's needs.

Code

```
# django_project/settings.py
CSRF_TRUSTED_ORIGINS = ["http://localhost:3000"]  # new
```

As a final step commit our Blog work to Git.

Shell

```
(.venv) > git status
(.venv) > git add -A
(.venv) > git commit -m "Blog API setup"
```

Conclusion

And that's it! We have deliberately repeated several steps from our earlier examples so the pattern of creating a new Django project and then its API should start to feel more familiar. The models are are pure traditional Django but otherwise the URLs, views, and serializers all come from DRF. We added a detail endpoint to our API and started to explore the power of serializers.

The *Blog* API is completely functional for local use at this point however there is a big problem: anyone can update or delete an existing blog post! In other words, we do not have any permissions in place. In the next chapter we will learn how to apply permissions to protect our API.

[75]https://docs.djangoproject.com/en/4.0/ref/settings/#csrf-trusted-origins

Chapter 7: Permissions

Security is an important part of any website but it is doubly important with web APIs. Currently our *Blog* API allows anyone full access. There are no restrictions; any user can do anything which is extremely dangerous. For example, an anonymous user can create, read, update, or delete any blog post. Even one they did not create! Clearly we do not want this.

Django REST Framework ships with several out-of-the-box permissions settings that we can use to secure our API. These can be applied at a project-level, a view-level, or at any individual model level.

In this chapter we will explore all three and end up with a custom permission so that only the author of a blog post has the ability to update or delete it.

Project-Level Permissions

Django REST Framework has a host of configurations[76] that are namespaced inside a single Django setting called `REST_FRAMEWORK`. We already made one of those, AllowAny[77], explicit in the `django_project/settings.py` file.

---

[76]https://www.django-rest-framework.org/api-guide/settings/

[77]https://www.django-rest-framework.org/api-guide/permissions/#allowany

Code

```
# django_project/settings.py
REST_FRAMEWORK = {
    "DEFAULT_PERMISSION_CLASSES": [
        "rest_framework.permissions.AllowAny",   # new
    ],
}
```

There are actually four built-in project-level permissions settings we can use:

- AllowAny[78] - any user, authenticated or not, has full access
- IsAuthenticated[79] - only authenticated, registered users have access
- IsAdminUser[80] - only admins/superusers have access
- IsAuthenticatedOrReadOnly[81] - unauthorized users can view any page, but only authenticated users have write, edit, or delete privileges

Implementing any of these four settings requires updating the DEFAULT_PERMISSION_CLASSES setting and refreshing our web browser. That's it!

Let's switch to IsAuthenticated so only authenticated, or logged in, users can view the API. Update the django_project/settings.py file as follows:

---

[78] http://www.django-rest-framework.org/api-guide/permissions/#allowany

[79] http://www.django-rest-framework.org/api-guide/permissions/#isauthenticated

[80] http://www.django-rest-framework.org/api-guide/permissions/#isadminuser

[81] http://www.django-rest-framework.org/api-guide/permissions/#isauthenticatedorreadonly

Code

```
# django_project/settings.py
REST_FRAMEWORK = {
    "DEFAULT_PERMISSION_CLASSES": [
        "rest_framework.permissions.IsAuthenticated",  # new
    ],
}
```

If you refresh your web browser nothing changes because we are already logged in with our superuser account. It should be present in the upper right corner of your browsable API. To log out enter the admin at `http://127.0.0.1:8000/admin/` and click the "Log Out" link in the upper right corner.

If you go back to `http://127.0.0.1:8000/api/v1/` it displays an HTTP 403 Forbidden error since authentication credentials were not provided. That's what we want.

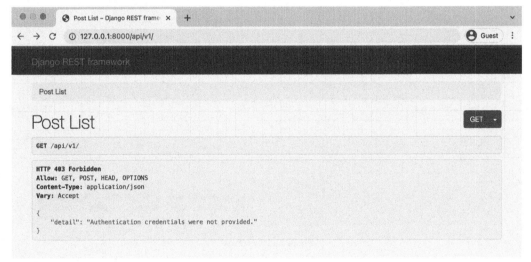

403 Error

Create New Users

We need to create a new user to test that a regular user–not just an admin superuser–has access to the API. There are two ways to do that: create a user in the command shell with `python` manage.py createsuperuser or we can log into the admin and add a user that way. Let's talk the admin route.

Head back to the admin at http://127.0.0.1:8000/admin/ and log in with your superuser credentials. Then click on "+ Add" next to Users. Enter a username and password for a new user and click on the "Save" button. I've chosen the username testuser here. Note the Name field is available but not required thanks to our custom user model.

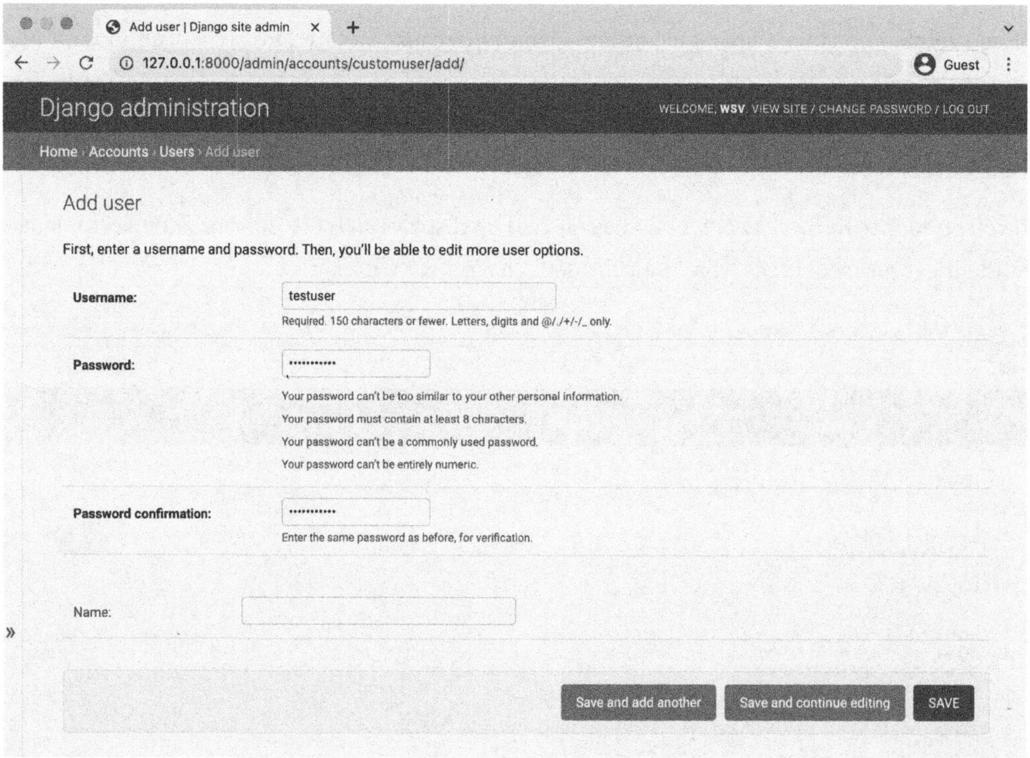

Admin Add User Page

The next screen is the Admin User Change page. I've called my user testuser and here I *could* add additional information included on the default User model such as first name, last name, email address, etc. But none of that is necessary for our purposes: we just need a username and password for testing.

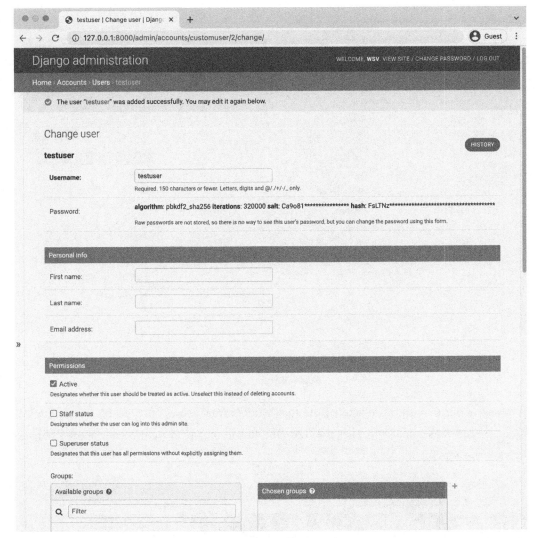

Admin User Change

Scroll down to the bottom of this page and click the "Save" button. It will redirect back to the main Users page at http://127.0.0.1:8000/admin/auth/user/[82].

---
[82]http://127.0.0.1:8000/admin/auth/user/

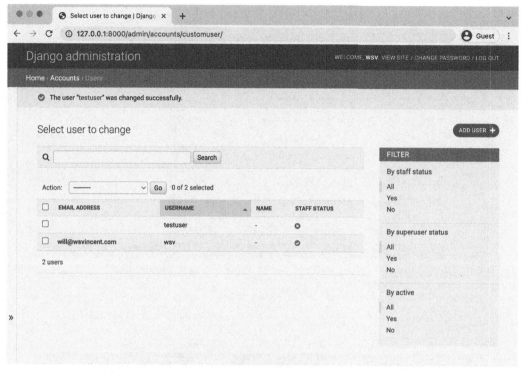

Admin Two Users

We can see our two users are listed. Note that "Staff Status" shows only one of the accounts is for a superuser. As a final step, click the "Log Out" link in the upper right corner of the webpage to leave the admin.

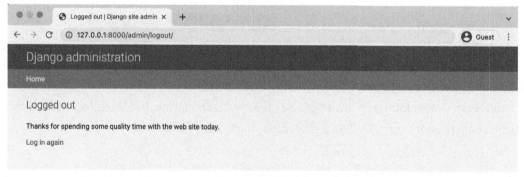

Admin Logout

Add Log In and Log Out

With that setup out of the way, how can our new user log in to the browsable API? We can do it by updating our project-level URLconf it turns out. Update `django_project/urls.py` as follows with the new path for log in.

Code

```
# django_project/urls.py
from django.contrib import admin
from django.urls import path, include


urlpatterns = [
    path("admin/", admin.site.urls),
    path("api/v1/", include("posts.urls")),
    path("api-auth/", include("rest_framework.urls")),  # new
]
```

Now navigate to our browsable API at `http://127.0.0.1:8000/api/v1/`. There is a subtle change: a "Log in" link in the upper right corner. Click on it to log in

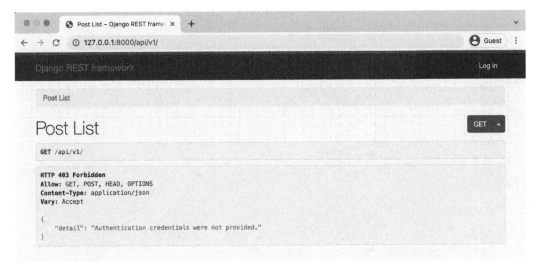

API Log In Link

Use the new `testuser` account to log in.

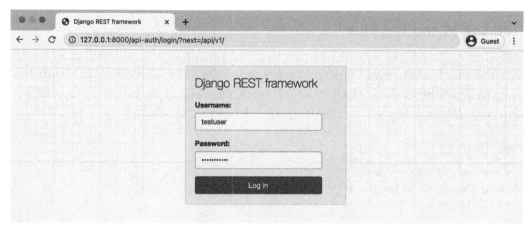

API Log In Page

This redirects back to the Post List page where `testuser` is present in the upper righthand corner along with an arrow that reveals a drop down "Log out" link.

API Log In Testuser

View-Level Permissions

Permissions can be added at the view-level too for more granular control. Let's update our
`PostDetail` view so that only admin users can view it. If we do this correctly, a logged out user
can't view the API at all, a logged-in user can view the list page, but only an admin can see the
detail page.

In the `posts/views.py` file import `permissions` from Django REST Framework and then add a permission_classes field to PostDetail that sets it to IsAdminUser.

Code

```
# posts/views.py
from rest_framework import generics, permissions   # new

from .models import Post
from .serializers import PostSerializer


class PostList(generics.ListCreateAPIView):
    queryset = Post.objects.all()
    serializer_class = PostSerializer


class PostDetail(generics.RetrieveUpdateDestroyAPIView):
    permission_classes = (permissions.IsAdminUser,)   # new
    queryset = Post.objects.all()
    serializer_class = PostSerializer
```

That's all we need. Refresh the browsable API at http://127.0.0.1:8000/api/v1/ and the Post List page is still viewable. However if you navigate to http://127.0.0.1:8000/api/v1/1/ to see the Post Detail page an HTTP 403 Forbidden status code is displayed.

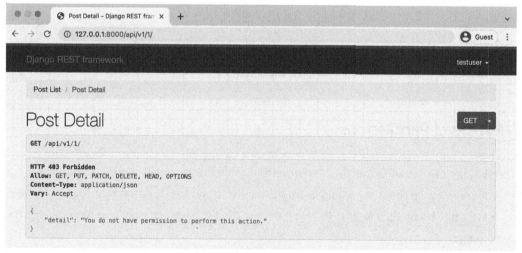

API Post Detail 403

If you log out of the browsable admin and then log in with your admin account the Post Detail page will still be visible. So we have effectively applied a view-level permission.

As you can see the standard types of permissions to set are allow any for full access, restrict to authenticated users, restrict to admin users, or allow authenticated users to perform any request but read-only for other users. How you configure permissions is dependent upon your project needs.

Before we proceed, remove the `permission_classes` field on `PostDetail`. For our purposes it is enough to restrict access to authenticated users which we've done in `django_project/settings.py` with the `DEFAULT_PERMISSION_CLASSES` configuration.

Custom Permissions

For our first custom permission we want to restrict access so that only the author of a blog post can edit it or delete it. The admin superuser will have access to do everything but a regular user can only update/delete their own content.

Internally, Django REST Framework relies on a `BasePermission` class from which all other permission classes inherit. All the built-in permissions settings like `AllowAny` or `IsAuthenticated` simple extend `BasePermission`. Here is the actual source code which is available on Github[83]:

Code

```
class BasePermission(object):
    """
    A base class from which all permission classes should inherit.
    """

    def has_permission(self, request, view):
        """
        Return `True` if permission is granted, `False` otherwise.
        """
        return True

    def has_object_permission(self, request, view, obj):
        """
        Return `True` if permission is granted, `False` otherwise.
```

---

[83]https://github.com/encode/django-rest-framework

```
    """
    return True
```

For a custom permission class you can override one or both of these methods. `has_permission` works on list views while detail views execute both: first `has_permission` and then, if that passes, `has_object_permission`. It is **strongly advised** to always set both methods explicitly because each defaults to `True`, meaning they will allow access implicitly unless set explicitly.

In our case, we want only the author of a blog post to have write permissions to edit or delete it. We also want to restrict read-only list view to authenticated users. To do this we'll create a new file called `posts/permissions.py` and fill it with the following code:

Code

```
# posts/permissions.py
from rest_framework import permissions


class IsAuthorOrReadOnly(permissions.BasePermission):
    def has_permission(self, request, view):
        # Authenticated users only can see list view
        if request.user.is_authenticated:
            return True
        return False

    def has_object_permission(self, request, view, obj):
        # Read permissions are allowed to any request so we'll always
        # allow GET, HEAD, or OPTIONS requests
        if request.method in permissions.SAFE_METHODS:
            return True

        # Write permissions are only allowed to the author of a post
        return obj.author == request.user
```

We import `permissions` at the top and then create a custom class `IsAuthorOrReadOnly` which extends `BasePermission`. The first method, `has_permission`, requires that a user be logged in, or authenticated, in order to have access. The second method, `has_object_permission`, allows read-only requests but limits write permissions to only the author of the blog post. We access the author field via `obj.author` and the current user with `request.user`.

Back in the `views.py` file we can remove the `permissions` import because we will swap out
`PostDetail`'s `permissions.IsAdminUser` in favor of importing our custom `IsAuthorOrReadOnly`
permission. Add the new permission to the `permission_classes` for both `PostDetail` and
`PostList`.

Code

```
# posts/views.py
from rest_framework import generics

from .models import Post
from .permissions import IsAuthorOrReadOnly   # new
from .serializers import PostSerializer


class PostList(generics.ListCreateAPIView):
    permission_classes = (IsAuthorOrReadOnly,)   # new
    queryset = Post.objects.all()
    serializer_class = PostSerializer


class PostDetail(generics.RetrieveUpdateDestroyAPIView):
    permission_classes = (IsAuthorOrReadOnly,)   # new
    queryset = Post.objects.all()
    serializer_class = PostSerializer
```

And we're done. To check this we need to create a blog post entry with `testuser` as the author
and confirm `testuser` can access it. Our current superuser account can see and do everything
by default. Navigate over to `http://127.0.0.1:8000/admin/` and log in as your superuser. Then
create a new post with `testuser` as the author.

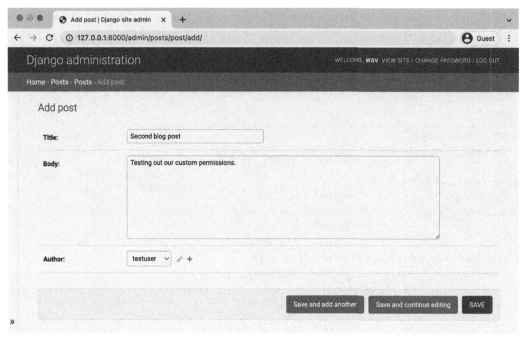

TestUser Post

After its creation head over to the Post Detail endpoint at `http://127.0.0.1:8000/api/v1/2/`.
Use the dropdown menu in the upper righthand corner to "Log out" of your superuser account
and log back in as `testuser`.

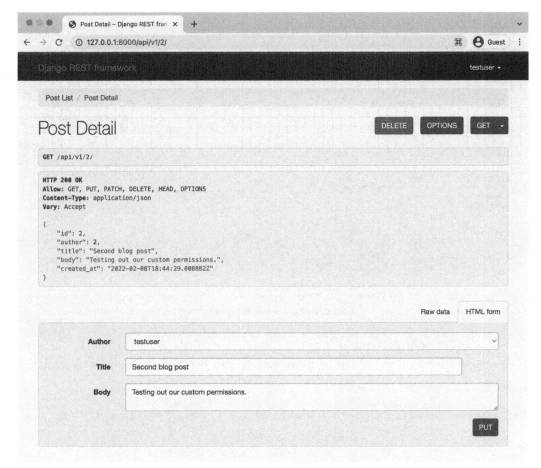

TestUser Post Detail

Yes! There are options to edit or delete the entry since `testuser` is the author. However if you navigate to the detail page for the first blog post at `http://127.0.0.1:8000/api/v1/1/` it is read-only since `testuser` was not the author.

TestUser Post Detail Not Author

To make sure our authentication controls work correctly log out in the upper right hand corner. Then navigate to both the Post List endpoint and the two Post Detail endpoints to confirm a logged out user does not have access.

To finish up we should commit our new work to Git.

Shell

```
(.venv) > git status
(.venv) > git add -A
(.venv) > git commit -m "add permissions"
```

Conclusion

Setting proper permissions is a very important part of any API. As a general strategy, it is a good idea to set a strict project-level permissions policy such that only authenticated users can view the API. Then make view-level or custom permissions more accessible as needed on specific API endpoints.

Chapter 8: User Authentication

In the previous chapter we updated our APIs permissions, which is also called **authorization**. In this chapter we will implement **authentication** which is the process by which a user can register for a new account, log in with it, and log out.

Within a traditional, monolithic Django website authentication is simpler and involves a session-based cookie pattern which we will review below. But with an API things are a bit trickier. Remember that HTTP is a **stateless protocol** so there is no built-in way to remember if a user is authenticated from one request to the next. Each time a user requests a restricted resource it must verify itself.

The solution is to pass along a unique identifier with each HTTP request. Confusingly, there is no universally agreed-upon approach for the form of this identifier and it can take multiple forms. Django REST Framework ships with four different built-in authentication options[84]: basic, session, token, and default. And there are many more third-party packages that offer additional features like JSON Web Tokens (JWTs).

In this chapter we will thoroughly explore how API authentication works, review the pros and cons of each approach, and then make an informed choice for our *Blog* API. By the end, we will have created API endpoints for sign up, log in, and log out.

Basic Authentication

The most common form of HTTP authentication is known as "Basic" Authentication[85]. When a client makes an HTTP request, it is forced to send an approved authentication credential before access is granted.

The complete request/response flow looks like this:

---

[84]https://www.django-rest-framework.org/api-guide/authentication/#api-reference
[85]https://tools.ietf.org/html/rfc7617

1. Client makes an HTTP request

2. Server responds with an HTTP response containing a `401 (Unauthorized)` status code and `WWW-Authenticate` HTTP header with details on *how* to authorize

3. Client sends credentials back via the Authorization[86] HTTP header

4. Server checks credentials and responds with either `200 OK` or `403 Forbidden` status code

Once approved, the client sends all future requests with the `Authorization` HTTP header credentials. We can also visualize this exchange as follows:

Diagram

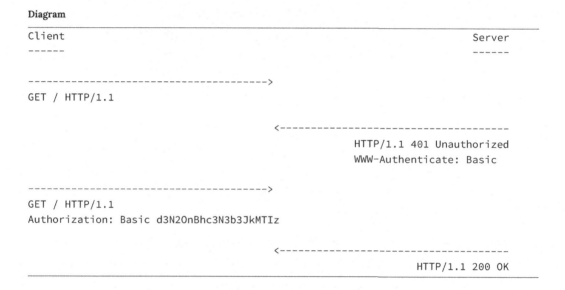

```
Client                                                                Server
------                                                                ------


--------------------------------------->
GET / HTTP/1.1


                            <---------------------------------------
                            HTTP/1.1 401 Unauthorized
                            WWW-Authenticate: Basic


--------------------------------------->
GET / HTTP/1.1
Authorization: Basic d3N2OnBhc3N3b3JkMTIz


                            <---------------------------------------
                                                    HTTP/1.1 200 OK
```

Note that the authorization credentials sent are the unencrypted base64 encoded[87] version of `<username>:<password>`. So in my case, this is `wsv:password123` which with base64 encoding is `d3N2OnBhc3N3b3JkMTIz`.

The primary advantage of this approach is its simplicity. But there are several major downsides. First, on *every single request* the server must look up and verify the username and password, which is inefficient. It would be better to do the look up once and then pass a token of some kind that says, this user is approved. Second, user credentials are being passed in clear text—not encrypted at all—over the internet. This is incredibly insecure. Any internet traffic that is not

---

[86]https://developer.mozilla.org/en-US/docs/Web/HTTP/Headers/Authorization
[87]https://en.wikipedia.org/wiki/Base64

encrypted can easily be captured and reused. Thus basic authentication should **only** be used via HTTPS[88], the secure version of HTTP.

Session Authentication

Monolithic websites, like traditional Django, have long used an alternative authentication scheme that is a combination of sessions and cookies. At a high level, the client authenticates with its credentials (username/password) and then receives a *session ID* from the server which is stored as a cookie. This session ID is then passed in the header of every future HTTP request.

When the session ID is passed, the server uses it to look up a session object containing all available information for a given user, including credentials.

This approach is **stateful** because a record must be kept and maintained on both the server (the session object) and the client (the session ID).

Let's review the basic flow:

1. A user enters their log in credentials (typically username/password)
2. The server verifies the credentials are correct and generates a session object that is then stored in the database
3. The server sends the client a session ID—not the session object itself—which is stored as a cookie on the browser
4. On all future requests the session ID is included as an HTTP header and, if verified by the database, the request proceeds
5. Once a user logs out of an application, the session ID is destroyed by both the client and server
6. If the user later logs in again, a new session ID is generated and stored as a cookie on the client

The default setting in Django REST Framework is actually a combination of Basic Authentication and Session Authentication. Django's traditional session-based authentication system is used and the session ID is passed in the HTTP header on each request via Basic Authentication.

---

[88]https://en.wikipedia.org/wiki/HTTPS

The advantage of this approach is that it is more secure since user credentials are only sent once, not on every request/response cycle as in Basic Authentication. It is also more efficient since the server does not have to verify the user's credentials each time, it just matches the session ID to the session object which is a fast look up.

There are several downsides however. First, a session ID is only valid within the browser where log in was performed; it will not work across multiple domains. This is an obvious problem when an API needs to support multiple front-ends such as a website and a mobile app. Second, the session object must be kept up-to-date which can be challenging in large sites with multiple servers. How do you maintain the accuracy of a session object across each server? And third, the cookie is sent out for every single request, even those that don't require authentication, which is inefficient.

As a result, it is generally not advised to use a session-based authentication scheme for any API that will have multiple front-ends.

Token Authentication

The third major approach–and the one we will implement in our *Blog* API–is to use token authentication. This is the most popular approach in recent years due to the rise of single page applications.

Token-based authentication is **stateless**: once a client sends the initial user credentials to the server, a unique token is generated and then stored by the client as either a cookie or in local storage[89]. This token is then passed in the header of each incoming HTTP request and the server uses it to verify that a user is authenticated. The server itself does not keep a record of the user, just whether a token is valid or not.

> **Cookies vs localStorage**
>
> Cookies are used for reading **server-side** information. They are smaller (4KB) in size and auto-matically sent with each HTTP request. LocalStorage is designed for **client-side** information. It is much larger (5120KB) and its contents are not sent by default with each HTTP request.

---

[89]https://developer.mozilla.org/en-US/docs/Web/API/Window/localStorage

> Tokens stored in both cookies and localStorage are vulnerable to XSS attacks. The current best practice is to store tokens in a cookie with the httpOnly and Secure cookie flags.

Let's look at a simple version of actual HTTP messages in this challenge/response flow. Note that the HTTP header WWW-Authenticate specifies the use of a Token which is used in the response Authorization header request.

Diagram

```
Client                                                  Server
------                                                  ------

-------------------------------------->
GET / HTTP/1.1

                          <-------------------------------------
                                    HTTP/1.1 401 Unauthorized
                                    WWW-Authenticate: Token

-------------------------------------->
GET / HTTP/1.1
Authorization: Token 401f7ac837da42b97f613d789819ff93537bee6a

                          <-------------------------------------
                                                HTTP/1.1 200 OK
```

There are multiple benefits to this approach. Since tokens are stored on the client, scaling the servers to maintain up-to-date session objects is no longer an issue. And tokens can be shared amongst multiple front-ends: the same token can represent a user on the website and the same user on a mobile app. The same session ID can not be shared amongst different front-ends, a major limitation.

A potential downside is that tokens can grow quite large. A token contains all user information, not just an id as with a session id/session object set up. Since the token is sent on every request, managing its size can become a performance issue.

Exactly *how* the token is implemented can also vary substantially. Django REST Frameworks' built-in TokenAuthentication[90] is deliberately quite basic. As a result, it does not support setting tokens to expire, which is a security improvement that can be added. It also only generates one token per user, so a user on a website and then later a mobile app will use the same token. Since information about the user is stored locally, this can cause problems with maintaining and updating two sets of client information.

JSON Web Tokens (JWTs) are a newer form of token containing cryptographically signed JSON data. JWTs were originally designed for use in OAuth[91], an open standard way for websites to share access to user information without actually sharing user passwords. JWTs can be generated on the server with a third-party package like djangorestframework-simplejwt[92] or via a third-party service like Auth0. There is an ongoing debate, however, among developers on the pros and cons of using JWTs for user authentication and covering it properly is beyond the scope of this book. That is why we will stick to the built-in TokenAuthentication in this book.

Default Authentication

The first step is to configure our new authentication settings. Django REST Framework comes with a number of settings[93] that are implicitly set. For example, DEFAULT_PERMISSION_CLASSES was set to AllowAny before we updated it to IsAuthenticated.

The DEFAULT_AUTHENTICATION_CLASSES are set by default so let's explicitly add both SessionAuthenticatio and BasicAuthentication to our django_project/settings.py file.

---

[90]http://www.django-rest-framework.org/api-guide/authentication/#tokenauthentication
[91]https://en.wikipedia.org/wiki/OAuth
[92]https://github.com/jazzband/djangorestframework-simplejwt
[93]http://www.django-rest-framework.org/api-guide/settings/

Code

```
# django_project/settings.py
REST_FRAMEWORK = {
    "DEFAULT_PERMISSION_CLASSES": [
        "rest_framework.permissions.IsAuthenticated",
    ],
    "DEFAULT_AUTHENTICATION_CLASSES": [   # new
        "rest_framework.authentication.SessionAuthentication",
        "rest_framework.authentication.BasicAuthentication",
    ],
}
```

Why use both methods? The answer is they serve different purposes. Sessions are used to power the Browsable API and the ability to log in and log out of it. BasicAuthentication is used to pass the session ID in the HTTP headers for the API itself.

If you revisit the browsable API at `http://127.0.0.1:8000/api/v1/` it will work just as before. Technically, nothing has changed, we've just made the default settings explicit.

Implementing token authentication

Now we need to update our authentication system to use tokens. The first step is to update our `DEFAULT_AUTHENTICATION_CLASSES` setting to use `TokenAuthentication` as follows:

Code

```
# django_project/settings.py
REST_FRAMEWORK = {
    "DEFAULT_PERMISSION_CLASSES": [
        "rest_framework.permissions.IsAuthenticated",
        ],
    "DEFAULT_AUTHENTICATION_CLASSES": [
        "rest_framework.authentication.SessionAuthentication",
        "rest_framework.authentication.TokenAuthentication",   # new
    ],
}
```

We keep `SessionAuthentication` since we still need it for our Browsable API, but now use tokens to pass authentication credentials back and forth in our HTTP headers. We also need to add the

authtoken app which generates the tokens on the server. It comes included with Django REST
Framework but must be added to our INSTALLED_APPS setting:

Code

```
# django_project/settings.py
INSTALLED_APPS = [
    "django.contrib.admin",
    "django.contrib.auth",
    "django.contrib.contenttypes",
    "django.contrib.sessions",
    "django.contrib.messages",
    "django.contrib.staticfiles",

    # 3rd-party apps
    "rest_framework",
    "corsheaders",
    "rest_framework.authtoken",  # new

    # Local
    "accounts.apps.AccountsConfig",
    "posts.apps.PostsConfig",
]
```

Since we have made changes to our INSTALLED_APPS we need to sync our database. Stop the
server with Control+c. Then run the following command.

Shell

```
(.venv) > python manage.py migrate
Operations to perform:
  Apply all migrations: accounts, admin, auth, authtoken, contenttypes, posts, sessions
Running migrations:
  Applying authtoken.0001_initial... OK
  Applying authtoken.0002_auto_20160226_1747... OK
  Applying authtoken.0003_tokenproxy... OK
```

Now start up the server again.

Shell

```
(.venv) > python manage.py runserver
```

If you navigate to the Django admin at `http://127.0.0.1:8000/admin/` you'll see there is now a `Tokens` section at the top. Make sure you're logged in with your superuser account to have access.

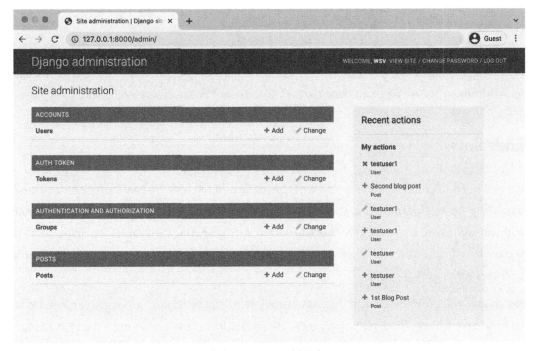

Admin Homepage with Tokens

Click on the link for `Tokens`. Currently there are no tokens which might be surprising.

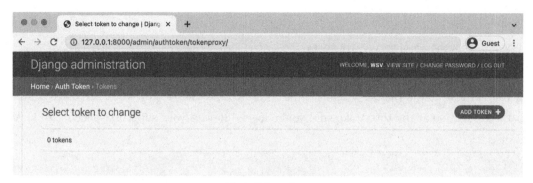

Admin Tokens Page

After all we have existing users. However, the tokens are only generated *after* there is an API call for a user to log in. We have not done that yet so there are no tokens. We will shortly!

Endpoints

We also need to create endpoints so users can log in and log out. We *could* create a dedicated users app for this purpose and then add our own urls, views, and serializers. However user authentication is an area where we really do not want to make a mistake. And since almost all APIs require this functionality, it makes sense that there are several excellent and tested third-party packages we can use instead.

Notably we will use dj-rest-auth[94] in combination with django-allauth[95] to simplify things. Don't feel bad about using third-party packages. They exist for a reason and even the best Django professionals rely on them all the time. There is no point in reinventing the wheel if you don't have to!

dj-rest-auth

First we will add log in, log out, and password reset API endpoints. These come out-of-the-box with the popular dj-rest-auth package. Stop the server with Control+c and then install it.

---

[94]https://github.com/jazzband/dj-rest-auth
[95]https://github.com/pennersr/django-allauth

Shell

```
(.venv) > python -m pip install dj-rest-auth==2.1.11
```

Add the new app to the INSTALLED_APPS config in our django_project/settings.py file.

Code

```
# django_project/settings.py
INSTALLED_APPS = [
    "django.contrib.admin",
    "django.contrib.auth",
    "django.contrib.contenttypes",
    "django.contrib.sessions",
    "django.contrib.messages",
    "django.contrib.staticfiles",

    # 3rd-party apps
    "rest_framework",
    "corsheaders",
    "rest_framework.authtoken",
    "dj_rest_auth",  # new

    # Local
    "accounts.apps.AccountsConfig",
    "posts.apps.PostsConfig",
]
```

Update our django_project/urls.py file with the dj_rest_auth package. We're setting the URL routes to api/v1/dj-rest-auth. Make sure to note that URLs should have a dash - not an underscore _, which is an easy mistake to make.

Code

```
# django_project/urls.py
from django.contrib import admin
from django.urls import path, include

urlpatterns = [
    path("admin/", admin.site.urls),
    path("api/v1/", include("posts.urls")),
    path("api-auth/", include("rest_framework.urls")),
    path("api/v1/dj-rest-auth/", include("dj_rest_auth.urls")),  # new
]
```

And we're done! If you have ever tried to implement your own user authentication endpoints, it is truly amazing how much time—and headache—dj-rest-auth saves for us. Now we can spin up the server to see what dj-rest-auth has provided.

Shell

```
(.venv) > python manage.py runserver
```

We have a working log in endpoint at http://127.0.0.1:8000/api/v1/dj-rest-auth/login/.

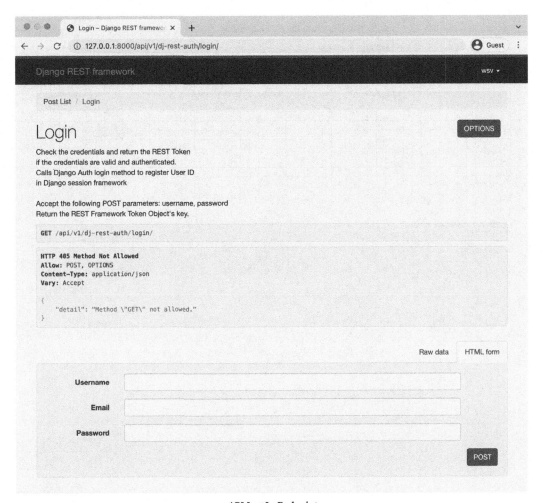

API Log In Endpoint

And a log out endpoint at `http://127.0.0.1:8000/api/v1/dj-rest-auth/logout/`.

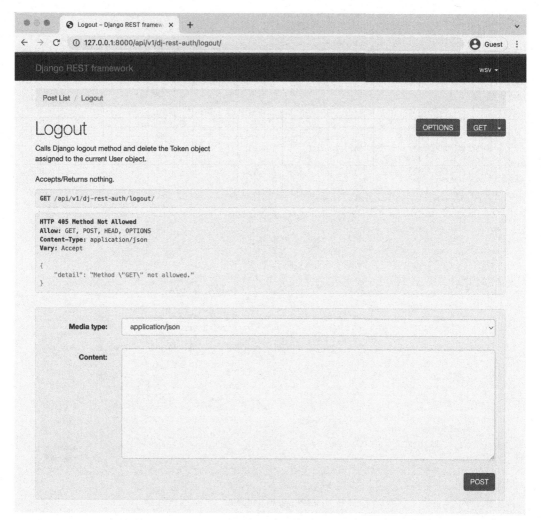

API Log Out Endpoint

There are also endpoints for password reset, which is located at:

```
http://127.0.0.1:8000/api/v1/dj-rest-auth/password/reset
```

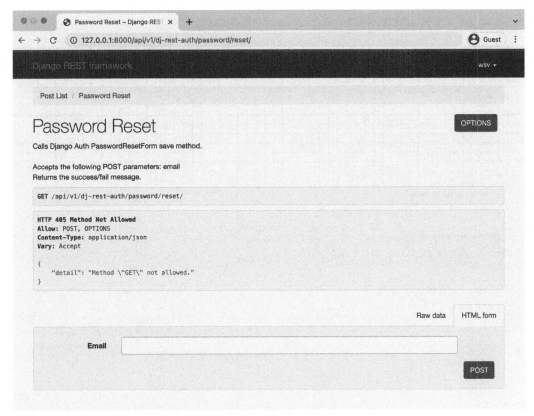

API Password Reset

And for password reset confirmed:

```
http://127.0.0.1:8000/api/v1/dj-rest-auth/password/reset/confirm
```

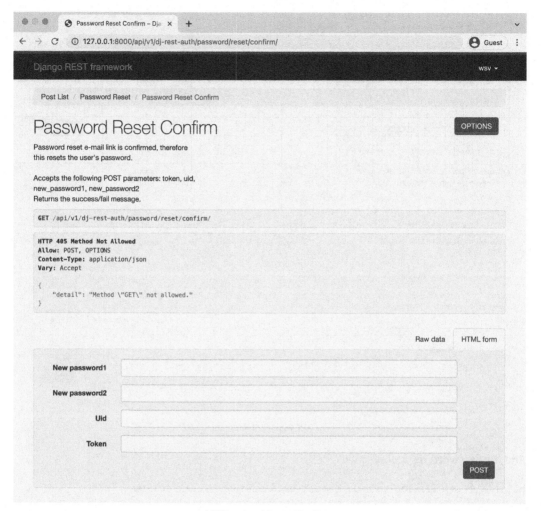

API Password Reset Confirm

User Registration

Next up is our user registration, or sign up, endpoint. Traditional Django does not ship with built-in views or URLs for user registration and neither does Django REST Framework. Which means we need to write our own code from scratch; a somewhat risky approach given the seriousness–and security implications–of getting this wrong.

A popular approach is to use the third-party package django-allauth[96] which comes with user registration as well as a number of additional features to the Django auth system such as social authentication via Facebook, Google, Twitter, etc. If we add `dj_rest_auth.registration` from the `dj-rest-auth` package then we have user registration endpoints too!

Stop the local server with `Control+c` and install `django-allauth`.

Shell

```
(.venv) > python -m pip install django-allauth~=0.48.0
```

Then update our `INSTALLED_APPS` setting. We must add several new configs:

- `django.contrib.sites`
- `allauth`
- `allauth.account`
- `allauth.socialaccount`
- `dj_rest_auth.registration`

Code

```python
# django_project/settings.py
INSTALLED_APPS = [
    "django.contrib.admin",
    "django.contrib.auth",
    "django.contrib.contenttypes",
    "django.contrib.sessions",
    "django.contrib.messages",
    "django.contrib.staticfiles",
    "django.contrib.sites",  # new

    # 3rd-party apps
    "rest_framework",
    "corsheaders",
    "rest_framework.authtoken",
    "allauth",  # new
    "allauth.account",  # new
    "allauth.socialaccount",  # new
    "dj_rest_auth",
```

---

[96]https://github.com/pennersr/django-allauth

```
    "dj_rest_auth.registration",  # new

    # Local
    "accounts.apps.AccountsConfig",
    "posts.apps.PostsConfig",
]
```

django-allauth needs to be added to the TEMPLATES configuration after existing context processors as well as setting the EMAIL_BACKEND to console and adding a SITE_ID of 1.

Code

```
# django_project/settings.py
TEMPLATES = [
    {
        "BACKEND": "django.template.backends.django.DjangoTemplates",
        "DIRS": [],
        "APP_DIRS": True,
        "OPTIONS": {
            "context_processors": [
                "django.template.context_processors.debug",
                "django.template.context_processors.request",
                "django.contrib.auth.context_processors.auth",
                "django.contrib.messages.context_processors.messages",
                "django.template.context_processors.request",  # new
            ],
        },
    },
]

EMAIL_BACKEND = "django.core.mail.backends.console.EmailBackend"  # new

SITE_ID = 1  # new
```

The email back-end config is needed since by default an email will be sent when a new user is registered, asking them to confirm their account. Rather than also set up an email server, we will output the emails to the console with the console.EmailBackend setting.

SITE_ID is part of the built-in Django "sites" framework[97], which is a way to host multiple websites from the same Django project. We only have one site we are working on here but django-allauth uses the sites framework, so we must specify a default setting.

---

[97]https://docs.djangoproject.com/en/4.0/ref/contrib/sites/

Ok. We've added new apps so it's time to update the database.

Shell

```
(.venv) > python manage.py migrate
```

Then add a new URL route for registration.

Code

```
# django_project/urls.py
from django.contrib import admin
from django.urls import path, include

urlpatterns = [
    path("admin/", admin.site.urls),
    path("api/v1/", include("posts.urls")),
    path("api-auth/", include("rest_framework.urls")),
    path("api/v1/dj-rest-auth/", include("dj_rest_auth.urls")),
    path("api/v1/dj-rest-auth/registration/",  # new
         include("dj_rest_auth.registration.urls")),
]
```

And we're done. We can run the local server.

Shell

```
(.venv) > python manage.py runserver
```

There is now a user registration endpoint at:

```
http://127.0.0.1:8000/api/v1/dj-rest-auth/registration/.
```

Tokens

To make sure everything works, create a third user account via the new user registration endpoint. I've called my user testuser1.

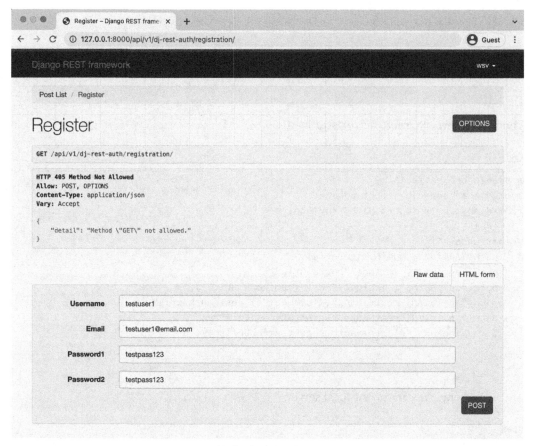

API Register New User

After clicking on the "POST" button the next screen shows the HTTP response from the server. Our user registration POST was successful, hence the status code HTTP 201 Created at the top. The return value key is the auth token for this new user.

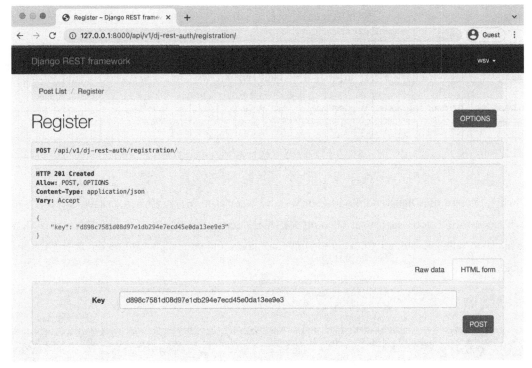

API Auth Key

If you look at the command line console, an email has been automatically generated by `django-allauth`. This default text can be updated and an email SMTP server added with additional configuration that is covered in the book *Django for Beginners*.

Shell

```
Content-Type: text/plain; charset="utf-8"
MIME-Version: 1.0
Content-Transfer-Encoding: 7bit
Subject: [example.com] Please Confirm Your E-mail Address
From: webmaster@localhost
To: testuser1@email.com
Date: Wed, 09 Feb 2022 16:22:38 -0000
Message-ID:
 <164442375878.25521.7693193428490319037@1.0.0.0.0.0.0.0.0.0.0.0.0.0.0.0.0.0.0.0.0.0.0.0.0.0.0.0.\
0.0.0.0.0.0.0.0.ip6.arpa>

Hello from example.com!
```

```
You're receiving this e-mail because user testuser1 has given your e-mail address to regi\
ster an account on example.com.

To confirm this is correct, go to http://127.0.0.1:8000/api/v1/dj-rest-auth/registration/\
account-confirm-email/MQ:1nHpjq:D1vZokltkCU2bqKO_g9cmA_hf2fThyl6vgtC7CpNdfI/

Thank you for using example.com!
example.com
------------------------------------------------------------------------
[09/Feb/2022 16:22:38] "POST /api/v1/dj-rest-auth/registration/ HTTP/1.1" 201 7828
```

Switch over to the Django admin in your web browser at `http://127.0.0.1:8000/admin/`. You
will need to use your superuser account for this. There are a number of new fields here that
`django-allauth` has added. Click on the link for `Tokens` and you will be redirected to the Tokens
page.

Admin Tokens

A single token has been generated by Django REST Framework for the `testuser1` user. As
additional users are created via the API, their tokens will appear here, too.

A logical question is, Why are there are no tokens for our superuser account or `testuser`? The
answer is that we created those accounts before token authentication was added. But no worries,
once we log in with either account via the API a token will automatically be added and available.

Moving on, let's log in with our new `testuser1` account. Make sure to log out of the admin and
then in your web browser navigate to `http://127.0.0.1:8000/api/v1/dj-rest-auth/login/`.
Enter the information for our `testuser1` account. Click on the "POST" button.

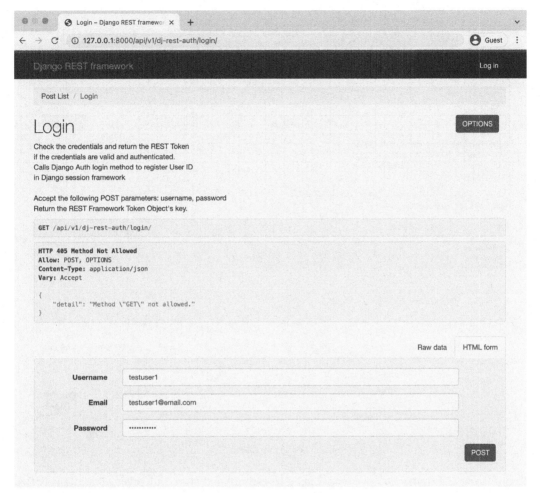

API Log In testuser1

Two things have happened. In the upper righthand corner, our user account `testuser1` is visible, confirming that we are now logged in. Also the server has sent back an HTTP response with the token.

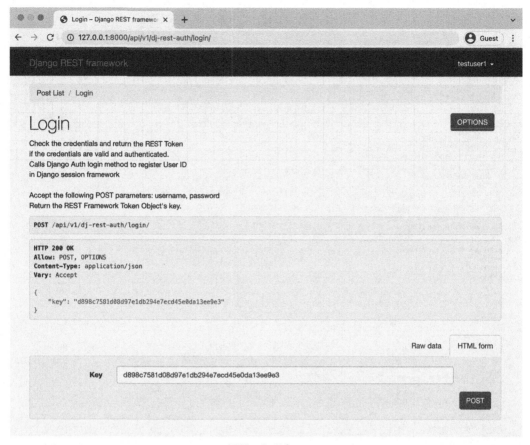

API Log In Token

In our front-end framework, we would need to capture and store this token. Traditionally this happens on the client, either in localStorage[98] or as a cookie, and then all future requests include the token in the header as a way to authenticate the user. Note that there are additional security concerns on this topic so you should take care to implement the best practices of your front-end framework of choice.

To finish up we should commit our new work to Git.

---

[98]https://developer.mozilla.org/en-US/docs/Web/API/Window/localStorage

Shell

```
(.venv) > git status
(.venv) > git add -A
(.venv) > git commit -m "add user authentication"
```

Conclusion

User authentication is one of the hardest areas to grasp when first working with web APIs. Without the benefit of a monolithic structure, we as developers have to deeply understand and configure our HTTP request/response cycles appropriately.

Django REST Framework comes with a lot of built-in support for this process, including built-in `TokenAuthentication`. However developers must configure additional areas like user registration and dedicated urls/views themselves. As a result, a popular, powerful, and secure approach is to rely on the third-party packages `dj-rest-auth` and `django-allauth` to minimize the amount of code we have to write from scratch.

Chapter 9: Viewsets and Routers

Viewsets[99] and routers[100] are tools within Django REST Framework that can speed-up API development. They are an additional layer of abstraction on top of views and URLs. The primary benefit is that a single viewset can replace multiple related views. And a router can automatically generate URLs for the developer. In larger projects with many endpoints this means a developer has to write less code. It is also, arguably, easier for an experienced developer to understand and reason about a small number of viewset and router combinations than a long list of individual views and URLs.

In this chapter we will add two new API endpoints to our existing project and see how switching from views and URLs to viewsets and routers can achieve the same functionality with far less code.

User endpoints

Currently we have the following API endpoints in our project. They are all prefixed with `api/v1/` which is not shown for brevity:

---

[99]http://www.django-rest-framework.org/api-guide/viewsets/
[100]http://www.django-rest-framework.org/api-guide/routers/

Diagram

```
|Endpoint                          |HTTP Verb|
|----------------------------------|---------|
|/                                 |GET      |
|/:pk/                             |GET      |
|/rest-auth/registration           |POST     |
|/rest-auth/login                  |POST     |
|/rest-auth/logout                 |GET      |
|/rest-auth/password/reset         |POST     |
|/rest-auth/password/reset/confirm |POST     |
```

The first two endpoints were created by us while `dj-rest-auth` provided the five others. Let's now add two additional endpoints to list all users and individual users. This is a common feature in many APIs and it will make it clearer why refactoring our views and URLs to viewsets and routers can make sense.

The process to wire up new endpoints *always* involves the following three steps:

- new serializer class for the model
- new views for each endpoint
- new URL routes for each endpoint

Start with our serializer. We need to import the `CustomUser` model and then create a `UserSerializer` class that uses it. Then add it to our existing `posts/serializers.py` file.

Code

```python
# posts/serializers.py
from django.contrib.auth import get_user_model  # new
from rest_framework import serializers

from .models import Post


class PostSerializer(serializers.ModelSerializer):

    class Meta:
        model = Post
        fields = ("id", "author", "title", "body", "created_at",)
```

```
class UserSerializer(serializers.ModelSerializer): # new

    class Meta:
        model = get_user_model()
        fields = ("id", "username",)
```

It's worth noting that while we have used `get_user_model` to reference the `CustomUser` model here, there are actually three different ways to reference[101] the current User model in Django.

By using `get_user_model` we ensure that we are referring to the correct user model, whether it is the default `User` or a custom user model[102] like `CustomUser` in our case.

Moving on we need to define views for *each* endpoint. First add `UserSerializer` to the list of imports. Then create both a `UserList` class that lists out all users and a `UserDetail` class that provides a detail view of an individual user. Just as with our `post` views we can use `ListCreateAPIView` and `RetrieveUpdateDestroyAPIView` here. We also need to reference the users model via `get_user_model` so it is imported on the top line.

Code

```
# posts/views.py
from django.contrib.auth import get_user_model  # new
from rest_framework import generics

from .models import Post
from .permissions import IsAuthorOrReadOnly
from .serializers import PostSerializer, UserSerializer  # new


class PostList(generics.ListCreateAPIView):
    permission_classes = (IsAuthorOrReadOnly,)
    queryset = Post.objects.all()
    serializer_class = PostSerializer


class PostDetail(generics.RetrieveUpdateDestroyAPIView):
    permission_classes = (IsAuthorOrReadOnly,)
    queryset = Post.objects.all()
    serializer_class = PostSerializer
```

---

[101]https://docs.djangoproject.com/en/4.0/topics/auth/customizing/#referencing-the-user-model
[102]https://docs.djangoproject.com/en/4.0/topics/auth/customizing/#specifying-a-custom-user-model

```
class UserList(generics.ListCreateAPIView):  # new
    queryset = get_user_model().objects.all()
    serializer_class = UserSerializer


class UserDetail(generics.RetrieveUpdateDestroyAPIView):  # new
    queryset = get_user_model().objects.all()
    serializer_class = UserSerializer
```

If you notice, there is quite a bit of repetition here. Both Post views and User views have the *exact same* queryset and serializer_class. Maybe those could be combined in some way to save code?

Finally we have our URL routes. Make sure to import our new UserList, and UserDetail views. Then we can use the prefix users/ for each.

Code

```
# posts/urls.py
from django.urls import path

from .views import PostList, PostDetail, UserList, UserDetail    # new

urlpatterns = [
    path("users/", UserList.as_view()),  # new
    path("users/<int:pk>/", UserDetail.as_view()),  # new
    path("", PostList.as_view()),
    path("<int:pk>/", PostDetail.as_view()),
]
```

And we're done. Make sure the local server is running and jump over to the browsable API to confirm everything works as expected.

Our user list endpoint is located at http://127.0.0.1:8000/api/v1/users/.

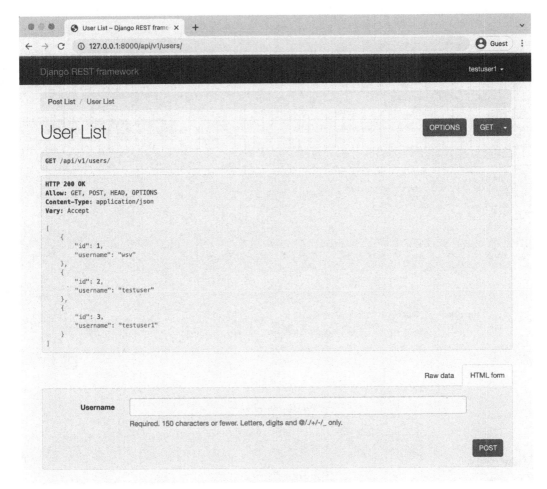

API Users List

The status code is `200 OK` which means everything is working. We can see our three existing users. A user detail endpoint is available at the primary key for each user. So our superuser account is located at: `http://127.0.0.1:8000/api/v1/users/1/`.

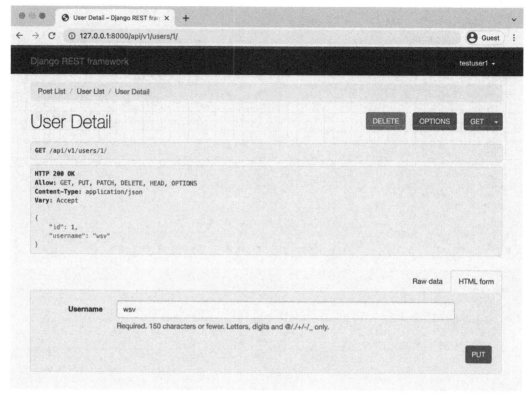

API User Instance

Viewsets

A viewset is a way to combine the logic for multiple related views into a single class. In other words, one viewset can replace multiple views. Currently we have four views: two for blog posts and two for users. We can instead mimic the same functionality with two viewsets: one for blog posts and one for users. The trade-off is that there is a loss in readability for fellow developers who are *not* intimately familiar with viewsets.

Here is what the code looks like in our updated posts/views.py file when we swap in viewsets.

Code

```
# posts/views.py
from django.contrib.auth import get_user_model
from rest_framework import viewsets  # new

from .models import Post
from .permissions import IsAuthorOrReadOnly
from .serializers import PostSerializer, UserSerializer


class PostViewSet(viewsets.ModelViewSet):  # new
    permission_classes = (IsAuthorOrReadOnly,)
    queryset = Post.objects.all()
    serializer_class = PostSerializer


class UserViewSet(viewsets.ModelViewSet):  # new
    queryset = get_user_model().objects.all()
    serializer_class = UserSerializer
```

At the top instead of importing `generics` from `rest_framework` we are now importing `viewsets` on the second line. Then we are using ModelViewSet[103] which provides both a list view and a detail view for us. And we no longer have to repeat the same `queryset` and `serializer_class` for each view as we did previously!

At this point, the local web server will stop as Django complains about the lack of corresponding URL paths. Let's set those next.

Routers

Routers[104] work directly with viewsets to automatically generate URL patterns for us. Our current `posts/urls.py` file has four URL patterns: two for blog posts and two for users. We can instead adopt a single route for each viewset. So two routes instead of four URL patterns. That sounds better, right?

---

[103]http://www.django-rest-framework.org/api-guide/viewsets/#modelviewset
[104]http://www.django-rest-framework.org/api-guide/routers/

Django REST Framework has two default routers: SimpleRouter[105] and DefaultRouter[106]. We will use `SimpleRouter` but it's also possible to create custom routers for more advanced functionality.

Here is what the updated code looks like:

Code

```
# posts/urls.py
from django.urls import path
from rest_framework.routers import SimpleRouter

from .views import UserViewSet, PostViewSet

router = SimpleRouter()
router.register("users", UserViewSet, basename="users")
router.register("", PostViewSet, basename="posts")

urlpatterns = router.urls
```

On the top line `SimpleRouter` is imported, along with our views. The `router` is set to `SimpleRouter` and we "register" each viewset for `Users` and `Posts`. Finally, we set our URLs to use the new router. Go ahead and check out our four endpoints now by starting the local server with `python manage.py runserver`. First up is `User List` at `http://127.0.0.1:8000/api/v1/users/` which is the same.

The detail view at `http://127.0.0.1:8000/api/v1/users/1/` is a little different though. It is now called "User Instance" instead of "User Detail" and there is an additional "delete" option which is built-in to ModelViewSet[107].

---

[105] http://www.django-rest-framework.org/api-guide/routers/#simplerouter
[106] http://www.django-rest-framework.org/api-guide/routers/#defaultrouter
[107] http://www.django-rest-framework.org/api-guide/viewsets/#modelviewset

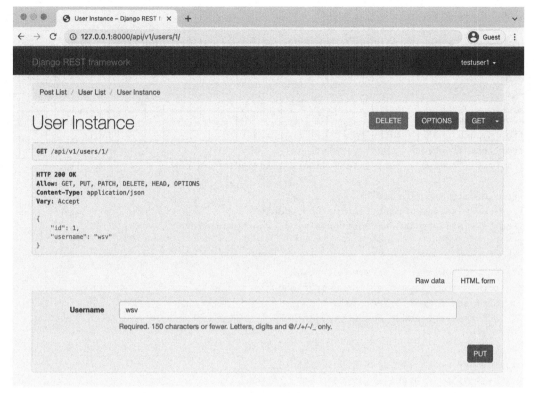

API User Detail

Permissions

If we stop and consider our API at the moment there is actually a huge security issue. Any authenticated user can add a new user on the User List page or edit/delete/update an individual on the User Instance page because there are no explicit permissions for `UserViewSet`. This is a big problem!

It is important to think of permissions for any API endpoint but especially when user information is involved. In this case, we want to restrict access to superusers only. If we look at the Permissions page in the official documentation there is an existing permissions setting called IsAdminUser[108] which is what we want. Adding it to the `UserViewSet` is actually pretty

---

[108]https://www.django-rest-framework.org/api-guide/permissions/#isadminuser

straightforward.

In the posts/views.py file import IsAdminUser at the top and then, under the UserViewSet class,
set permission_classes to [IsAdminUser].

Code

```
# posts/views.py
from django.contrib.auth import get_user_model
from rest_framework import viewsets
from rest_framework.permissions import IsAdminUser   # new

from .models import Post
from .permissions import IsAuthorOrReadOnly
from .serializers import PostSerializer, UserSerializer


class PostViewSet(viewsets.ModelViewSet):
    permission_classes = (IsAuthorOrReadOnly,)
    queryset = Post.objects.all()
    serializer_class = PostSerializer


class UserViewSet(viewsets.ModelViewSet):
    permission_classes = [IsAdminUser]  # new
    queryset = get_user_model().objects.all()
    serializer_class = UserSerializer
```

The local web server should automatically restart with the changed code so we can revist the
User List endpoint at http://127.0.0.1:8000/api/v1/users/.

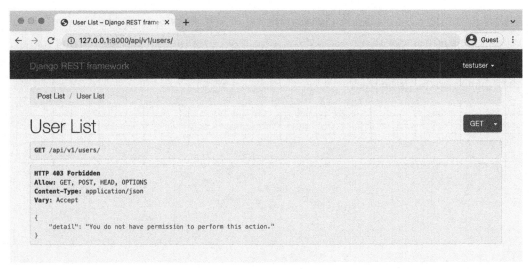

User List Admin Only

Even though we are still logged in as `testuser` this endpoint is unavailable and the same is true for each User Instance endpoint.

When setting permissions it is always a good idea to have restrictive project-level settings and open up access per endpoint as needed. It is also important to check that existing endpoints are not left wide open, as our Users were earlier, which is quite easy to do!

To finish up we should commit our new work to Git.

Shell

```
(.venv) > git status
(.venv) > git add -A
(.venv) > git commit -m "add schema and documentation"
```

Conclusion

Viewsets and routers are a powerful abstraction that reduce the amount of code we as developers must write. However this conciseness comes at the cost of an initial learning curve. It will feel strange the first few times you use viewsets and routers instead of views and URL patterns.

Ultimately the decision of *when* to add viewsets and routers to your project is subjective. A good rule of thumb is to start with views and URLs. As your API grows in complexity if you find yourself repeating the same endpoint patterns over and over again, then look to viewsets and routers. Until then, keep things simple.

Chapter 10: Schemas and Documentation

Now that we have our API complete we need a way to document its functionality quickly and accurately to others. After all, in most companies and teams, the developer who is using the API is not the same developer who initially built it. And if an API is available to the public it definitely needs a well-documented guide to be usable.

A **schema** is a machine-readable document that outlines all available API endpoints, URLs, and the HTTP verbs (GET, POST, PUT, DELETE, etc.). This is great but not very readable for a human. Enter **documentation** which is something added to a schema that makes it easier for humans to read and consume.

As a reminder, here is the complete list of our current API endpoints:

Diagram

Endpoint	HTTP Verb
/	GET
/:pk/	GET
users/	GET
users/:pk/	GET
/rest-auth/registration	POST
/rest-auth/login	POST
/rest-auth/logout	GET
/rest-auth/password/reset	POST
/rest-auth/password/reset/confirm	POST

In this chapter we will add both machine-readable schema and human-readable documentation to our *Blog* project. Even better, we will automate the generation of each so that they are always up-to-date with the latest version of our API.

Schema

The OpenAPI[109] specification is the current default way to document an API. It describes common rules around format for available endpoints, inputs, authentication methods, contact information, and more. As of this writing, drf-spectacular[110] is the recommended third-party package for generating an OpenAPI 3 schema for Django REST Framework.

To start, install `drf-spectacular` with Pip in the usual way.

Shell

```
(.venv) > python -m pip install drf-spectacular~=0.21.0
```

Add it to the INSTALLED_APPS configuration in the `django_project/settings.py` file.

Code

```
# django_project/settings.py
INSTALLED_APPS = [
    "django.contrib.admin",
    "django.contrib.auth",
    "django.contrib.contenttypes",
    "django.contrib.sessions",
    "django.contrib.messages",
    "django.contrib.staticfiles",
    "django.contrib.sites",

    # 3rd-party apps
    "rest_framework",
    "corsheaders",
    "rest_framework.authtoken",
    "allauth",
    "allauth.account",
    "allauth.socialaccount",
    "dj_rest_auth",
    "dj_rest_auth.registration",
    "drf_spectacular",  # new

    # Local
    "accounts.apps.AccountsConfig",
```

---

[109]https://www.openapis.org/
[110]https://github.com/tfranzel/drf-spectacular/

```
        "posts.apps.PostsConfig",
]
```

Then register drf-spectacular within the REST_FRAMEWORK section of the django_project/settings.py file.

Code

```
# django_project/settings.py
REST_FRAMEWORK = {
    "DEFAULT_PERMISSION_CLASSES": [
        "rest_framework.permissions.IsAuthenticated",
        ],
    "DEFAULT_AUTHENTICATION_CLASSES": [
        "rest_framework.authentication.SessionAuthentication",
        "rest_framework.authentication.TokenAuthentication",
    ],
    "DEFAULT_SCHEMA_CLASS": "drf_spectacular.openapi.AutoSchema",  # new
}
```

The last step is adding some metadata such as title, description, and version to the default settings[111]. Create a new section in django_project/settings.py and add the following:

Code

```
# django_project/settings.py
SPECTACULAR_SETTINGS = {
    "TITLE": "Blog API Project",
    "DESCRIPTION": "A sample blog to learn about DRF",
    "VERSION": "1.0.0",
    # OTHER SETTINGS
}
```

To generate the schema as a standalone file we can use a management command and specify the name of the file, which will be schema.yml.

---

[111]https://drf-spectacular.readthedocs.io/en/latest/settings.html

Shell

```
(.venv) > python manage.py spectacular --file schema.yml
```

A new `schema.yml` file has been created in the project-root directory. If you open that file in your text editor it's quite long and not very human-friendly. But to a computer it's perfectly formatted.

Dynamic Schema

A more dynamic approach is to serve the schema directly from our API as a URL route. We'll do this by importing `SpectacularAPIView` and then adding a new URL path at `api/schema/` to display it.

Code

```python
# django_project/urls.py
from django.contrib import admin
from django.urls import path, include
from drf_spectacular.views import SpectacularAPIView  # new


urlpatterns = [
    path("admin/", admin.site.urls),
    path("api/v1/", include("posts.urls")),
    path("api-auth/", include("rest_framework.urls")),
    path("api/v1/dj-rest-auth/", include("dj_rest_auth.urls")),
    path(
        "api/v1/dj-rest-auth/registration/",
        include("dj_rest_auth.registration.urls"),
    ),
    path("api/schema/", SpectacularAPIView.as_view(), name="schema"),  # new
]
```

Start up the local server again with `python manage.py runserver` and navigate to the new schema URL endpoint at `http://127.0.0.1:8000/api/schema/`. The automatically generated schema file of our entire API is available and will be downloaded as a file.

Personally, I prefer the dynamic approach in projects rather than having to regenerate a `schema.yml` file each time there is an API change.

Documentation

A schema is well and good for consumption by a computer but humans generally prefer documentation for using an API. There are two API documentation tools supported by drf-spectacular: Redoc[112] and SwaggerUI[113]. Fortunately transforming our schema into either is a relatively painless process.

Let's begin with Redoc. To add it import SpectacularRedocView at the top of django_project/urls.py and then add a URL path at api/schema/redoc/.

Code

```
# django_project/urls.py
from django.contrib import admin
from django.urls import path, include
from drf_spectacular.views import (
    SpectacularAPIView,
    SpectacularRedocView,  # new
)


urlpatterns = [
    path("admin/", admin.site.urls),
    path("api/v1/", include("posts.urls")),
    path("api-auth/", include("rest_framework.urls")),
    path("api/v1/dj-rest-auth/", include("dj_rest_auth.urls")),
    path("api/v1/dj-rest-auth/registration/",
        include("dj_rest_auth.registration.urls")
    ),
    path("api/schema/", SpectacularAPIView.as_view(), name="schema"),
    path("api/schema/redoc/", SpectacularRedocView.as_view(
        url_name="schema"), name="redoc",),  # new
]
```

If the local server is still running you can head directly to http://127.0.0.1:8000/api/schema/redoc/ to see our new documentation.

---

[112]https://redoc.ly/redoc/
[113]https://swagger.io/tools/swagger-ui/

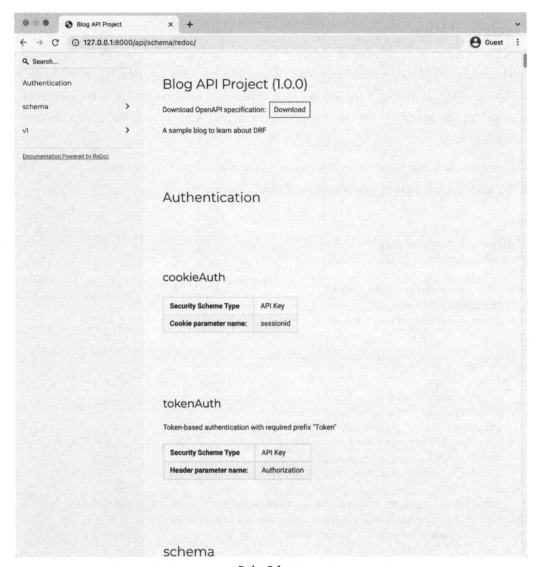

Redoc Schema

The process for adding SwaggerUI is quite similar. Import `SpectacularSwaggerView` at the top of the file and then add a URL path for it at `api/schema/swagger-ui/`.

Code

```
# django_project/urls.py
from django.contrib import admin
from django.urls import path, include
from drf_spectacular.views import (
    SpectacularAPIView,
    SpectacularRedocView,
    SpectacularSwaggerView,  # new
)


urlpatterns = [
    path("admin/", admin.site.urls),
    path("api/v1/", include("posts.urls")),
    path("api-auth/", include("rest_framework.urls")),
    path("api/v1/dj-rest-auth/", include("dj_rest_auth.urls")),
    path("api/v1/dj-rest-auth/registration/",
        include("dj_rest_auth.registration.urls")
    ),
    path("api/schema/", SpectacularAPIView.as_view(), name="schema"),
    path("api/schema/redoc/", SpectacularRedocView.as_view(
        url_name="schema"), name="redoc",),
    path("api/schema/swagger-ui/", SpectacularSwaggerView.as_view(
        url_name="schema"), name="swagger-ui"),  # new
]
```

Then head over to the web browser to see the output at:

`http://127.0.0.1:8000/api/schema/swagger-ui/.`

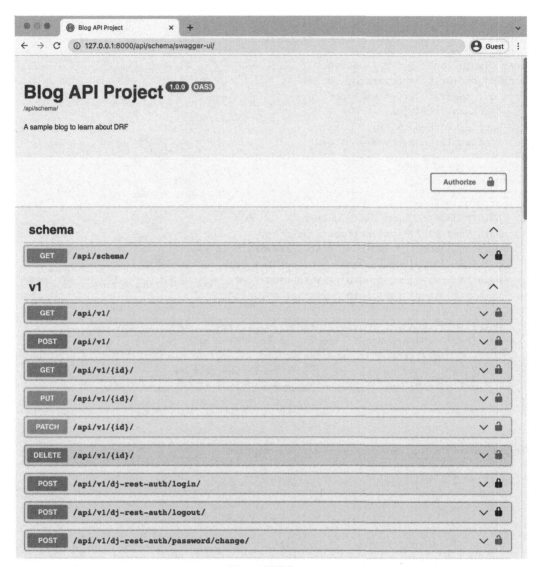

SwaggerUI Schema

Conclusion

Adding a schema and documentation is a vital part of any API. It is typically the first thing a fellow developer looks at, either within a team or on an open-source projects. Thanks to the automated tools covered in this chapter, ensuring your API has accurate, up-to-date documentation only requires a small amount of configuration. The last step is to deploy the Blog API properly which we'll cover in the next chapter.

Chapter 11: Production Deployment

The final step for any web API project is deployment. Pushing it into production is very similar to a traditional Django deployment but with some added concerns. In this chapter, we will cover adding environment variables, configuring our settings to be more secure, switching to a PostgreSQL database in production, and running through Django's own deployment checklist to make sure we are not missing anything.

Environment Variables

Environment variables can be loaded into a codebase at runtime yet not stored in the source code. This makes them an ideal way to toggle between local and production settings. They are also a good place to store sensitive information that should not be present in source control. When using Git, any changes are stored in the Git history, so even if something is later removed from the codebase, if it was checked into a commit at any time it is there forever if someone knows how to look.

There are multiple packages that enable working with environment variables in Python but for this project we'll use environs[114] because it comes with an additional Django configuration that is very useful.

Let's begin by installing `environs[django]`. If you are using Zsh as your terminal shell it is necessary to add single quotes, `''`, around the package name, so run `python -m pip install 'environs[django]==9.3.5'`.

---

[114]https://github.com/sloria/environs

Shell

```
(.venv) > python -m pip install 'environs[django]==9.5.0'
```

There are three lines of imports to add near the top of the django_project/settings.py file.

Code

```
# django_project/settings.py
from pathlib import Path
from environs import Env  # new

env = Env()  # new
env.read_env()  # new
```

Then create a new hidden file called .env in the root project directory which will store our environment variables. It is empty for now but will be used in the next section. The last step is to add .env to our existing .gitignore file. There's no sense using environment variables if they will still be stored in Git!

.gitignore

```
.venv/
.env
```

And while we are updating the file we might as well as add all *.pyc files and the __pycache__-directory. If you're on a Mac, there's no need to track .DS_Store which stores information about folder settings. Finally, it is not a good idea to commit the local db.sqlite3 to source control. It contains the entire database so anyone with access to all our data. We will continue to use it locally for convenience and see shortly how PostgreSQL can be used in production instead.

Here is what the final .gitignore file should contain:

.gitignore

```
.venv/
.env
__pycache__/
db.sqlite3
.DS_Store  # Mac only
```

Before committing run `git status` to confirm all these files are being ignored as intended. Then add our new work and create a commit.

Shell

```
(.venv) > git status
(.venv) > git add -A
(.venv) > git commit -m "add environment variables"
```

DEBUG & SECRET_KEY

Django's default `settings.py` file automatically defaults to local production settings that make it easy to start with projects, but there are several configurations that need to be tweaked before deploying into production. If you look at the `DEBUG` configuration in `django_project/settings.py` it is currently set to `True`. This generates a very detailed error page and stack trace. For example, start up the local webserver with `python manage.py runserver` and visit an API endpoint that doesn't exist such as `http://127.0.0.1:8000/99`.

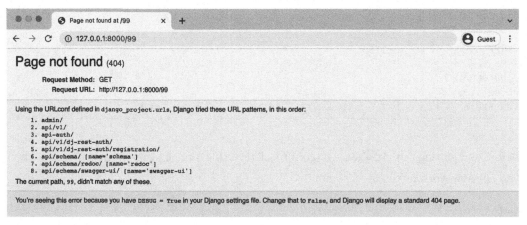

404 Page

We want DEBUG to be True for local development yet False for production. And if there is any difficulty loading the environment variables, we want DEBUG to default to False so we're extra secure. To implement this, start by adding DEBUG=True to the .env file.

.env

```
DEBUG=True
```

Then in django_project/settings.py, change the DEBUG setting to read the variable "DEBUG" from the .env file but with a default value of False.

Code

```
# django_project/settings.py
DEBUG = env.bool("DEBUG", default=False)
```

If you refresh the webpage at http://127.0.0.1:8000/99, you'll see the full local error page is still there. Everything is working properly.

The next setting to change is SECRET_KEY which is a random 50 character string generated each time startproject is run. If you look at the current value in django_project/settings.py it starts with django-insecure to indicate the current value is not secure. Why is it insecure? Because it is easy to commit the SECRET_KEY to source control as, in fact, we have already done. Even if we moved the current value into an environment variable now it will still remain visible in the project's Git history.

The solution is to generate a new secret key and to store that value in an environment variable so it never touches source control. One way to generate a new one is by invoking Python's built-in secrets[115] module by running `python -c 'import secrets; print(secrets.token_urlsafe())'` on the command line.

Shell

```
(.venv) > python -c "import secrets; print(secrets.token_urlsafe())"
KBl3sX5kLrd2zxj-pAichjT0EZJKMS0cXzhWI7Cydqc
```

Copy and paste this new value into the `.env` file under the variable `SECRET_KEY`.

.env

```
DEBUG=True
SECRET_KEY=KBl3sX5kLrd2zxj-pAichjT0EZJKMS0cXzhWI7Cydqc
```

Finally, switch over `SECRET_KEY` in the `django_project/settings.py` file to read from the environment variable now.

Code

```
# django_project/settings.py
SECRET_KEY = env.str("SECRET_KEY")
```

To confirm everything is working properly restart the local server with `python manage.py runserver` and refresh any API endpoint on our site. It should be working normally.

ALLOWED HOSTS

Next up is the `ALLOWED_HOSTS` configuration in our `django_project/settings.py` file which represents the host/domain names our Django project can serve. We will add three hosts here: `.herokuapp.com` for the deployment on Heroku and both `localhost` and `127.0.0.1` for local development.

---

[115]https://docs.python.org/3/library/secrets.html

Code

```
# django_project/settings.py
ALLOWED_HOSTS = [".herokuapp.com", "localhost", "127.0.0.1"]  # new
```

If you re-run the `python manage.py runserver` command and refresh `http://127.0.0.1:8000/1`
it should display normally after the change.

DATABASES

Our current `DATABASES` configuration is for SQLite but we want to be able to switch to PostgreSQL
for production on Heroku. When we installed `environs[django]` earlier, the Django "goodies"
included the elegant dj-database-url[116] package, which takes all the database configurations
needed for our database, SQLite or PostgreSQL, and creates a `DATABASE_URL` environment
variable.

To implement this update the `DATABASES` configuration with `dj_db_url` from `environs[django]`
to help parse `DATABASE_URL`.

Code

```
# django_project/settings.py
DATABASES = {
    "default": env.dj_db_url("DATABASE_URL")  # new
}
```

That's it! All we need to do now is specify SQL as the local `DATABASE_URL` value in the `.env` file.

.env

```
DEBUG=True
SECRET_KEY=KBl3sX5kLrd2zxj-pAichjT0EZJKMS0cXzhWI7Cydqc
DATABASE_URL=sqlite:///db.sqlite3
```

This seems quite magical, no? The reason it works is because whenever Heroku provisions a new
PostgreSQL database it automatically creates a configuration variable for it named `DATABASE_URL`.
Since the `.env` file is not committed to production, our Django project on Heroku will instead
use this PostgreSQL configuration. Pretty elegant, no?

---

[116]https://github.com/jacobian/dj-database-url

Static Files

As we saw in earlier deployments static files need to be configured for the browsable web API to work. First, create a new project-level directory called `static`.

Shell

```
(.venv) > mkdir static
```

With your text editor create an empty `.keep` file within the `static` directory so it is picked up by Git. Then install `whitenoise` to handle static files in production.

Shell

```
(.venv) > python -m pip install whitenoise==5.3.0
```

WhiteNoise must be added to `django_project/settings.py` in the following locations:

- `whitenoise` above `django.contrib.staticfiles` in `INSTALLED_APPS`
- `WhiteNoiseMiddleware` above `CommonMiddleware`
- `STATICFILES_STORAGE` configuration pointing to WhiteNoise

Code

```python
# django_project/settings.py
INSTALLED_APPS = [
    ...
    "whitenoise.runserver_nostatic",  # new
    "django.contrib.staticfiles",
]

MIDDLEWARE = [
    "django.middleware.security.SecurityMiddleware",
    "django.contrib.sessions.middleware.SessionMiddleware",
    "whitenoise.middleware.WhiteNoiseMiddleware",  # new
    "corsheaders.middleware.CorsMiddleware",
    ...
]

STATIC_URL = "/static/"
```

```
STATICFILES_DIRS = [str(BASE_DIR.joinpath("static"))]  # new
STATIC_ROOT = str(BASE_DIR.joinpath("staticfiles"))  # new
STATICFILES_STORAGE =
    "whitenoise.storage.CompressedManifestStaticFilesStorage"  # new
```

The final step is to run the `collectstatic` command so that all static directories and files are compiled into one location for deployment purposes.

Shell

```
(.venv) > python manage.py collectstatic
```

Pyscopg and Gunicorn

There are two final packages that must be installed for a proper production environment. Psycopg[117] is a database adapter that lets Python apps talk to PostgreSQL databases. If you are on macOS it is necessary to install PostgreSQL first via Homebrew and then `psycopg2`.

Shell

```
# Windows
(.venv) > python -m pip install psycopg2==2.9.3

# macOS
(.venv) % brew install postgresql
(.venv) % python -m pip install psycopg2==2.9.3
```

We can use this approach because Django's ORM (Object Relational Mapper) translates our `models.py` code from Python into the database backend of choice. This works *almost* all the time without error. It is possible for weird bugs to creep up and it is recommended on a professional project to install PostgreSQL locally, too, to avoid them.

Gunicorn is a production web server and must be installed as well to replace the current Django web server which is only suitable for local development.

---

[117]https://www.psycopg.org/docs/

Shell

```
(.venv) > python -m pip install gunicorn==20.1.0
```

requirements.txt

As we have seen before in this book, a requirements.txt file is needed which lists all the packages installed in our local virtual environment. We can do that as well with the following command.

Shell

```
(.venv) > python -m pip freeze > requirements.txt
```

Here is what the contents of my requirements.txt file look like. Yours might look slightly different: for example, Django will likely be on a 4.1.1 or later release because we installed it using ~= which means the latest 4.0.x version is installed.

requirements.txt

```
asgiref==3.5.0
attrs==21.4.0
certifi==2021.10.8
cffi==1.15.0
charset-normalizer==2.0.11
cryptography==36.0.1
defusedxml==0.7.1
dj-database-url==0.5.0
dj-email-url==1.0.5
dj-rest-auth==2.1.11
Django==4.0.2
django-allauth==0.48.0
django-cache-url==3.2.3
django-cors-headers==3.10.1
djangorestframework==3.13.1
drf-spectacular==0.21.2
environs==9.5.0
gunicorn==20.1.0
idna==3.3
inflection==0.5.1
jsonschema==4.4.0
```

```
marshmallow==3.14.1
oauthlib==3.2.0
psycopg2==2.9.3
pycparser==2.21
PyJWT==2.3.0
pyrsistent==0.18.1
python-dotenv==0.19.2
python3-openid==3.2.0
pytz==2021.3
PyYAML==6.0
requests==2.27.1
requests-oauthlib==1.3.1
sqlparse==0.4.2
uritemplate==4.1.1
urllib3==1.26.8
whitenoise==5.3.0
```

Procfile and runtime.txt

Heroku relies on a custom file called Procfile that describes how to run projects in production. This must be created in the project root directory next to the manage.py file. Do so now in your text editor and add the following line to use Gunicorn as the production web server.

Procfile

```
web: gunicorn django_project.wsgi --log-file -
```

The final step is to specify which Python version should run on Heroku with a runtime.txt file. In your text editor, create this new runtime.txt file at the project-level meaning it is in the same directory as manage.py and the Procfile. The Python version we want is 3.10.2.

runtime.txt

```
python-3.10.2
```

Deployment Checklist

We just went through a lot of steps. Too many to remember for most developers which is why deployment checklists exist. To recap, here is what we did:

- add environment variables via `environs[django]`
- set `DEBUG` to `False`
- set `ALLOWED_HOSTS`
- use environment variable for `SECRET_KEY`
- update `DATABASES` to use SQLite locally and PostgreSQL in production
- configure static files and install `whitenoise`
- install `gunicorn` for a production web server
- create a `requirements.txt` file
- create a `Procfile` for Heroku
- create a `runtime.txt` to set the Python version on Heroku

Aside from the `Procfile` file created for Heroku these deployment steps are virtually the same for any hosting platform.

Make sure to commit all these changes to Git before we actually deploy the project.

Shell

```
(.venv) > git status
(.venv) > git add -A
(.venv) > git commit -m "deployment checklist"
```

Heroku Deployment

To deploy on Heroku make sure you are logged in via the terminal shell.

Shell

```
(.venv) > heroku login
```

The command `heroku create` makes a new container for our app to live in and by default, Heroku will assign a random name. You can specify a custom name, as we are doing here, but it must be *unique on Heroku*. Mine is called `dfa-blog-api` so that name is already taken; you need another combination of letters and numbers!

Shell

```
(.venv) > heroku create dfa-blog-api
Creating ⬚ dfa-blog-api... done
https://dfa-blog-api.herokuapp.com/ | https://git.heroku.com/dfa-blog-api.git
```

So far so good. A new step at this point is creating a PostgreSQL database on Heroku itself, which we haven't done before. Heroku has its own hosted PostgreSQL databases we can use which come in multiple tiers. For a learning project like this, the free `hobby-dev` tier is more than adequate. Run the following command to create this new database. Replace `dfa-blog-api` with your own custom name.

Shell

```
(.venv) > heroku addons:create heroku-postgresql:hobby-dev -a dfa-blog-api
Creating heroku-postgresql:hobby-dev on ⬚ dfa-blog-api... free
Database has been created and is available
 ! This database is empty. If upgrading, you can transfer
 ! data from another database with pg:copy
Created postgresql-angular-74744 as DATABASE_URL
Use heroku addons:docs heroku-postgresql to view documentation
```

Did you see that Heroku has created a custom `DATABASE_URL` to access the database? For mine here, it is `postgresql-angular-74744`. This is automatically available as a configuration variable within Heroku once we deploy. That's why we don't need to set an environment variable for `DATABASE_URL` in production. We also don't need to set `DEBUG` to `False` because that is the default value in our `django_project/settings.py` file. The only environment variable to manually add to Heroku is `SECRET_KEY`, so copy its value from your `.env` file and run the `config:set` command, placing the value of the `SECRET_KEY` itself within double quotes `""`.

Shell

```
(.venv) > heroku config:set SECRET_KEY="KBl3sX5kLrd2zxj-pAichjT0EZJKMS0cXzhWI7Cydqc"
Setting SECRET_KEY and restarting ▨ dfa-blog-api... done, v5
SECRET_KEY: KBl3sX5kLrd2zxj-pAichjT0EZJKMS0cXzhWI7Cydqc
```

Now it's time to push our code up to Heroku itself and start a web process so our Heroku dyno is running.

Shell

```
(.venv) > git push heroku main
(.venv) > heroku ps:scale web=1
```

The URL of your new app will be in the command line output or you can run `heroku open` to find it. We don't have a standard home page for this API so you need to travel to an endpoint like `/api/v1/`.

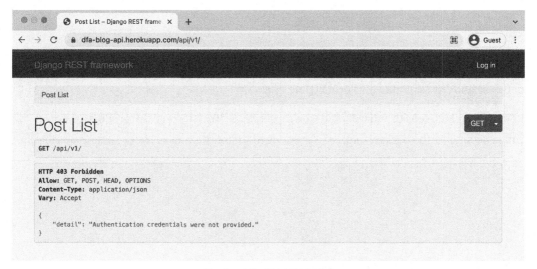

Deployed Post List Endpoint

If you click on the "Log in" link in the upper right corner it responds with a 500 Server Error message! That's because the PostgreSQL database exists but has not been setup yet!

500 Server Error

Previously we used SQLite in production, which is file-based, and was already configured locally and then pushed up to Heroku. But this PostgreSQL database of ours is brand new! Heroku has all our code but we haven't configured this production database yet.

The same process used locally of running `migrate`, creating a `superuser` account, and entering blog posts in the admin must be followed again. To run a command with Heroku, as opposed to locally, prefix it with `heroku run`.

Shell

```
(.venv) > heroku run python manage.py migrate
(.venv) > heroku run python manage.py createsuperuser
```

You will need to log into the live admin site to add blog entries and users since this is a brand-new database and not related to our local SQLite one.

Refresh your live website and it should work correctly. Note that since the production server will run constantly in the background, you do *not* need to use the `runserver` command on Heroku.

Conclusion

We're now at the end of the book but only the beginning of what can be accomplished with Django REST Framework. Over the course of three different projects–the *Library* API, *Todo* API, and *Blog* API–we have built, tested, and deployed progressively more complex web APIs from scratch. And it's no accident that at every step along the way, Django REST Framework provides built-in features to make our life easier.

If you've never built web APIs before with another framework be forewarned that you've been spoiled. And if you have, rest assured this book only scratches the surface of what Django REST Framework can do. The official documentation[118] is an excellent resource for further exploration now that you have a handle on the basics.

Advanced Topics

As a web API grows there are several additional topics worth exploring that we did not cover in the book. Pagination[119] is a helpful way to control how data is displayed on individual API endpoints. Filtering[120] also becomes necessary in many projects especially in conjunction with the excellent django-filter[121] library.

Throttling[122] is often necessary on APIs as a more advanced form of permissions. For example, the public-facing side of the API might have restrictive limits for unauthenticated requests while authenticated requests face much more lenient throttling.

The final additional area to explore is caching[123] of the API for performance reasons. This works in a very similar manner to how caching is handled on traditional Django projects.

---

[118] http://www.django-rest-framework.org/
[119] https://www.django-rest-framework.org/api-guide/pagination/
[120] https://www.django-rest-framework.org/api-guide/filtering/
[121] https://github.com/carltongibson/django-filter
[122] https://www.django-rest-framework.org/api-guide/throttling/
[123] https://www.django-rest-framework.org/api-guide/caching/

Next Steps

A good next step is to implement the pastebin API covered in the official DRF tutorial[124]. It should not be that difficult after completing this book and showcases a few more sides of DRF.

Third-party packages are as essential to Django REST Framework development as they are to Django itself. A complete listing can be found at Django Packages[125] or a curated list on the awesome-django[126] repo on Github.

Ultimately, how you proceed in using Django and Django REST Framework depends on what you want to build. Is the goal to integrate with a mobile iOS or Android app? To work in coordination with a full-blown JavaScript front-end? For internal use or to display public-facing content? The best way to learn is to work backwards from a big project and figure out the pieces along the way.

Giving Thanks

While the Django community is quite large and relies on the hard work of many individuals, Django REST Framework is much smaller in comparison. It was initially created by Tom Christie[127], an English software engineer who now works on it full-time thanks to open-source funding.

Thank you for reading along and supporting my work. If you purchased the book on Amazon, please consider leaving an honest review: they make an enormous impact on book sales and help me continue to produce both books and free Django content which I love doing.

---

[124]http://www.django-rest-framework.org/tutorial/1-serialization/
[125]https://djangopackages.org/
[126]https://github.com/wsvincent/awesome-django
[127]http://www.tomchristie.com/

Made in United States
Orlando, FL
18 March 2023

31171560R00115